On Scotland's Conscience

This book honours Professor Sir Robert Grieve, Sir Robert Cowan and the many unsung heroes who worked tirelessly to make the Highlands and Islands a better place. And those still doing that.

On Scotland's Conscience

The case for the Highlands and Islands

Edited by Iain MacDonald

KESSOCK BOOKS

First published in Great Britain by Kessock Books 2017
Copyright in this collection © Kessock Books 2017

A CIP catalogue record for this book is available from the British Library

ISBN 978-0-9930296-5-3

Cover design by Audiografix

Text design and typesetting by Stanford DTP

Printed and bound in Great Britain by CPI Group (UK)

Contents

Acknowledgements

We acknowledge the industry of Rab MacWilliam in seeing this work to fruition. Our thanks go to Wendy Price for allowing us to print on page xi the map she prepared for the 1995 HIE Annual Report. We are also grateful to Charlie King, John Hutchison, John Watt and David Ross, among others, for copy tasting and corrections. Any mistakes are acknowledged as our own.

About Kessock Books

Kessock Books was established in the summer of 2014 by a group of Highlanders who have been friends since their schooldays in Inverness.

We are an independent, small company, committed to publishing books on the Highlands and Islands. We cover a range of topics and themes from the light-hearted to the serious, and from the historical to the contemporary.

Although on occasion we adopt a sceptical approach to many of the legends, stories and myths which have been widely disseminated in and about the Highlands, all our books share a deep affection for this culturally diverse and fascinating region.

About the Editor

Iain MacDonald was born and brought up in the Western Isles and now lives in Inverness. For 35 years, he worked for BBC Scotland, mostly as a reporter in and about the Highlands and Islands.

Throughout those years, he has chronicled the efforts and experiences of the HIDB and HIE, interviewing those who have led the organisations, many of their officials and most of those to whom they have reported, in successive governments. He has never been a member of any political party.

About the Contributors

Maggie Cunningham is from the island of Scalpay. A fluent Gaelic speaker, she campaigned as a student for better representation for the language in the media. She then spent more than 20 years in broadcasting, becoming Station Manager at BBC Radio Highland in Inverness in 1992, before returning to the BBC in Glasgow, where she was to become Head of Programmes and Head of Radio for BBC Scotland. She was one of the leading figures in the establishment of the Gaelic television service BBC Alba, and went on to chair the new company. She was a founder member of Sistema Scotland, and is chief executive of Columba 1400, a social enterprise and charity for young people.

Michael Foxley is a crofter and retired GP. He is a former leader of The Highland Council, and a former board member of Bòrd na Gàidhlig, as well as chairing the regional board of the University of the Highlands and Islands and serving on the board of NHS Highland. He also chaired UHI's West Highland College. A local councillor representing Fort William and Ardnamurchan for over a quarter of a century, he became leader of Scotland's largest local authority (by land mass) in 2009. A land reform campaigner, he has frequently called for the end of all tax breaks for absentee landowners, and has been instrumental in community land buyouts in the west Highlands. He courted controversy when he announced he would vote 'yes' in the Scottish Independence Referendum in 2014.

Professor James Hunter hails from Argyll. His doctoral thesis *The Making of the Crofting Community* examined the history of land in the Highlands and Islands, from the point of view of those who had been cleared from their homes, a revolutionary approach for historians of that era. Forty years later it is still in print. He has published twelve books, his most recent, *Set Adrift Upon The World*, winning the Saltire Society's History prize. In the mid-1980s he became the founding Director of the Scottish Crofters' Union, today the Scottish Crofters' Federation. He served for six years as chairman of Highlands and Islands Enterprise. Throughout his career, he has campaigned for land reform. He was awarded a CBE in 2001. He was elected a Fellow of the Royal Society of Edinburgh in 2007. He is an SNP supporter.

Brian Wilson was founding editor and publisher of the radical newspaper, the *West Highland Free Press*, which he set up on the Isle of Skye, with a group of university friends, in 1971. He was elected MP for Cunningham North in 1987, and successfully defended the seat at three subsequent elections. As a Scottish Office minister with responsibility for the Highlands and Islands, he set up the Community Land Unit which helped secure community buyouts across the country, as well as becoming the first designated minister for Gaelic. He went on to become Trade Minister and Energy Minister in Labour administrations. In 2005, he became chairman of Harris Tweed Hebrides. His work for this industry won him Global Director of the Year Awards from the Institute of Directors. He was also the minister who appointed James Hunter chairman of HIE.

Our Board has tried to express within itself a simple aim—the aim of adding another perfectly possible way of life to that in the great cities.

Professor Robert Grieve

All that the HIDB has done is waste public money. But thank God that money's being wasted here.

Un-named Highland Regional councillor

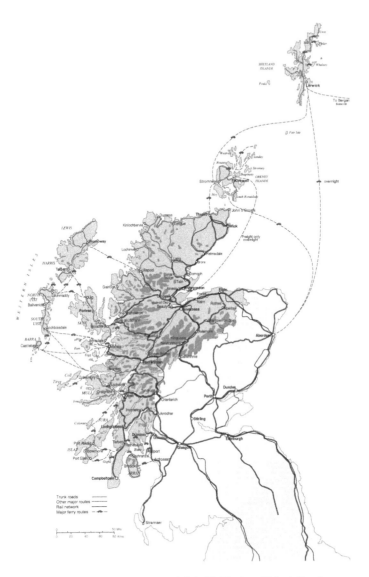

Highlands and Islands Enterprise succeeded the Highlands and Islands Development Board. Local Enterprise Companies were set up and, though Highland heads were sceptically shaken, they turned out to be a largely successful piece of Highland devolution. Crucially, though, the new HIE area was moved eastwards, across Nairn and Moray. Today, Highland Perthshire has also been added to the HIE area. How much damage has this done to the original Crofting Counties?

Introduction

'It cannot be a country… it is a torn saltire'

Iain MacDonald

Iain MacDonald, the Highland-based broadcaster, journalist and editor of this book, explains why a debate needs to take place about the Highlands and Islands' role in the new Scotland – and the Scottish government's role in the Highlands and Islands.

Most people know the Chinese curse: 'may you live in interesting times'. Today, we are certainly doing that. One only has to consider the UK's determined march out of the European Union and the election of a narcissistic man-child, with a crazy coiffure, to lead the Western world. Interesting times, indeed.

So, in these circumstances, why should anyone care about the fate of an agency located in the far north of the United Kingdom, tasked with the social and economic wellbeing of an under-occupied place of moors and mountains a million miles removed from such über-issues?

In this book, our four distinguished Highland voices should be able to answer that question. All have different views and political positions. But their analysis is remarkably similar on one issue. That issue is the continued existence of an autonomous, effective Highlands and Islands Enterprise.

On Scotland's Conscience borrows its title from the man who, in 1966, brought what was then the Highlands and Islands Development Board into existence. Secretary of State for Scotland Willie Ross told the House of Commons that, for 200 years, the Highlander had been the man – these were times less attuned to gender equalities – on Scotland's conscience.

This, after all, was a country – Scotland – and a population which had mostly stood by, or even turned away, as a succession of Highland communities were stripped of their people, some packed off to scrape a living on inhospitable coasts, some far over the sea to unknown lands. Yes, perhaps there should have been some guilt.

In order to assuage that conscience, therefore, here was the HIDB. Crucially, they were offered the tools and left to get on with the job. Their brief was both economic and social. In today's jargon, they were asked to apply holistic solutions to what was by then known as the Highland Problem.

Galloping depopulation was the worst of it. Young people went away for an education or training, and generally they stayed away. Because 'away' was where the work was. I am one of those people. I left my island home in 1967, just a year after the birth of the HIDB. I have not lived there since.

So, no doubt about the size of the job, nor indeed about its importance to the country. In an early interview, the first chair of HIDB Robert Grieve said this: 'Until this is done, and the Highlands becomes on its feet economically and socially, I don't think Scotland can really be whole. It cannot be a country.

'It is a torn saltire.'

Politics and Placemen

So did Grieve and his successors get the job done? Later in this book, one of his successors as chair of what was by then Highlands and Islands Enterprise, Professor James Hunter, will argue that yes it did – at least in part. But all our contributors will contend there is much still to be done, particularly in the more remote rural areas and islands away from the unquestionable prosperity of the Inner Moray Firth.

In this book, Peter Peacock, who formerly led Highland Council, before going on to become a Scottish government minister, marvels at how much independence of approach was demonstrated in Robert Grieve's first annual report for HIDB. But it would be foolish to pretend that, in the years that followed, there was no political influence from governments of the day.

There have been many who have sat in the chair first occupied by Robert Grieve, all of them appointed by the ruling party either at Westminster or Holyrood. SNP member Jim Hunter may have been given the job by Labour, but most of the others were political placemen. There has never been a woman in the top chair, which is not to the credit of the agency or its political masters.

But even some of those put in charge, on the grounds that they were politically reliable, have often 'gone native' and finished up as advocates for the Highlands to government, rather than the other way round. Prominent among these was Bob Cowan.

Sir Robert Cowan was appointed chair of HIDB in 1982. A native of Edinburgh who had made most of his career south of the border, he was by then director of a management consultant company based in Hong Kong. Highlanders thought so little of this appointment that he was locally dubbed 'Robert Co-Th'ann', a word which sounds much the same as his English language surname, but translates roughly as 'who him?'.

It was assumed he had been appointed as a Tory fellow traveller, (especially as his sister had gone to the same Oxford college as Margaret Thatcher). His early term of office coincided with the closure of the Invergordon smelter, with the loss of 1,000 jobs, in a facility set down in the Highlands as part of a previous government's policy of cultivating 'growth points'. Mr Cowan, later Sir Robert, wrestled with those problems, and emerged from that crisis as a man with changed political priorities.

I remember, as a working journalist, having my questions to the new chair about HIDB's social remit brusquely dismissed at his first press conference. Months later, at an HIDB drinks reception, he went out of his way to tell me that he now understood the notion of a social remit entirely. *Everything* we do here, he told me, has a social dimension.

And he wasn't afraid to fall out with his political masters, both in private and in public. In the 1980s, a new timber factory opened at Morayhill, near Inverness's airport at Dalcross, dedicated to a new product which had been christened Sterling Board.

HIDB had ploughed considerable government resources into the new factory, and both Sir Robert and the then Scottish Office minister Lord Gray of Contin were at the top table, apparently united for the occasion despite government threats to downsize the agency. Sir Robert rose to share details of the behind-the-scenes debate about the new product's name.

'We suggested it should be called Highland Board', he said, to much hilarity, as the minister glowered at his side, 'because it's so easy to cut.' This was a chair of HIDB – and its successor body HIE – prepared to fight for the Highlands and Islands because he lived and worked here and came to understand what was needed. His death at the age of 60 was much mourned.

Robert Cowan, like other chairs, left much work still to do. Will that work be done by an autonomous agency which knows its patch, and has the freedom to decide on the right solutions for the people and the area: an organisation discharging a social, as well as an economic function, and one unafraid to speak out? Maybe not.

Burying Bad News

We're familiar with the spin doctors' concept of a 'good day to bury bad news'. The notion came from a Labour adviser Jo

Moore, who wrote on '9/11' – 11 September 2001 – as people sat aghast before their television sets watching hijacked airliners being flown into New York's World Trade Centre Twin Towers, that it would be a good day to get 'anything out we want to bury'.

That much-pilloried precept may have been in play in the Holyrood Parliament on 23 November 2016. John Swinney, the Deputy First Minister and the Cabinet Secretary for Education and Skills, rose to make a statement, apparently on universities. It was the day of the first Autumn Statement by Theresa May's Chancellor Philip Hammond, and media attention was turned on Westminster. A day to bury bad news?

While on his feet, Mr Swinney slipped in the news that there was to be a shake-up. The government planned bringing together HIE, Scottish Enterprise, Skills Development Scotland, the Scottish Funding Council (which administers money for further and higher education) and a notional South of Scotland Enterprise. HIE, like the others, would lose its board, and the whole disparate mix would be run by what was described as an 'overarching' board, based presumably in the Central Belt. Initially, hardly anyone noticed Mr Swinney's announcement.

It was Rhoda Grant, a Highlands and Islands list MSP who had pursued the government relentlessly as it cut the HIE budget and staffing, who first spotted it. Soon, angry press releases were flying out to the Scottish media, though most newspapers had by then put their papers to bed. But a fire had been lit in the north.

The government had already faced the charge of control freakery from its political opponents. It had centralised all police and fire and rescue services, under new bodies – Police Scotland and Fire And Rescue Scotland – closing down Northern Constabulary and the Highland Fire Service, among others.

There had already been a series of rows about both of these, with armed police appearing on the streets of Inverness on routine patrols, while there were claims that the Fire Service control room, now moved out of the Highlands to Dundee, was sending crews hundreds of miles to the wrong places. Now, said the critics, here was more of the same.

Ministers, though, argued that the new organisation would bring skills and development bodies together, co-ordinating government activity more effectively. HIE, argued Keith Brown, the minister who had been handed this hot potato, would still be locally based, staffed and managed. International opportunities would be created.

Highlanders mostly haven't bought that. The area, many reckoned, would still be operating under a permanent Central Belt diktat, in contrast to the formerly autonomous HIDB. Though the SNP's MSPs and MPs have mostly stayed quiet in public, there were worried meetings with the minister. They were right to be worried.

On 18 January 2017, on the motion of a Conservative MSP who is the son of a clan chief, the government's plan was defeated by 64 votes to 63. Mr Brown promised to go away and think about it. Since then, a new report – drawn up for the government by HIE's current chair Lorne Crerar, a Glasgow lawyer with Gairloch connections, has suggested that HIE should get to keep its board. But it will still be subordinate to a centralised 'superboard'.

On The Move

HIDB and HIE have never really stood still. Indeed, they've never been able to. It is in the nature of politicians to tinker, and HIDB has experienced plenty of that.

The biggest sleight of hand came in 1991. Michael Forsyth, the MP for Stirling and a hard-line Thatcherite trouble-shooter, had been hunting HIDB's use of public funds through a series of parliamentary questions. Now, he was in the Scottish Office, and the agency was at his mercy.

Highlands and Islands Development Board swiftly became Highlands and Islands Enterprise, to deploy a Conservative buzz word. The new chairman was Fraser Morrison, an affable, Tory-supporting construction company boss. There was a new chief executive, the whip-smart minister's son Iain Robertson, recruited from an oil company. And, within a couple of years, there was a Local Enterprise Company network across the HIE area: companies composed mostly of local business people expected to provide extra added entrepreneurship. Highland heads shook in sorrowful scepticism.

Yet in just a few months the new system had bedded in, and even the LECs were regarded as a good thing, devolving, as they did, much of HIE's previously centralised powers and decision-making, even though the final word stayed with Inverness. HIE's bosses surprised people by governing the entire organisation with a generally light touch.

The system was to continue largely unchallenged, through the Blair years and devolution, until the SNP took power in 2007. It abolished the LECs, as part of a new Scottish Government Economic Strategy. They were to be replaced by what is described as 'a regional delivery model' for enterprise support, to cut bureaucracy and streamline local delivery. HIE's jobs responsibility through Business Gateway was transferred to local authorities.

Since then, HIE has visibly shrunk, both in terms of its budget and its staff. Numbers are sometimes hard to pin down, but it started with a £50 million cut soon after the new government took power. An estimated 60 jobs went early, reducing Inverness staffing to just over 100. Many of those who went were HIE's most experienced case officers and directors.

Other functions the agency used to fulfil have been chipped away or simply removed to other organisations. The mantra in recent years has been that HIE is a 'delivery organisation' and it funds only projects that they dub 'transformational', such as the University of the Highlands and Islands and life sciences company Inverness Medical. The small stuff: not so much.

Over the years, the organisation, too, has been constantly on the move – or, at least, its Inverness headquarters has. HIDB started life at Castle Wynd in Inverness town centre, then moved to Culduthel Road at the top of Castle Street – a building where I subsequently worked for BBC Scotland, who are still there today – then down to the riverside into one of the ugliest buildings ever to sully a city.

That Bridge Street behemoth is now a block of luxury flats, and HIE moved on in 2002, 30 years after it had moved in. Their new home was on the Inverness Retail Park, outside the city on the A96 road east, in a purpose-built block named after Sir Robert Cowan.

But in 2014, HIE was again on the move. They had to leave Cowan House to make way for a French financial technology company, which was promising to create 500 new jobs over three years as it moved into the Highlands. There was not much dignity to this enforced move.

HIE moved back into Inverness's city centre to a building formerly occupied by British Telecoms. A new headquarters has been built as part of the multi-million pound Univerity of the Highlands campus, once again on the edge of the city, in the Beechwood complex. But who knows who might next need that building for something transformational?

Kessock Books has not previously dipped its toes in political waters, partly because, as a company, we have no party preference. We believe, though, that it's part of our job, as a Highland-based book publisher, to identify issues in the area, and to provide a platform for others to speak out when there's something important at stake. We are essentially the bus, not the bus driver.

But we believe this is one of these issues, and we have assembled people who agree with us on its importance. You will find they can speak very well for themselves.

The future of the Highlands and Islands is in play. The outcome will be important to all of us in the north. We hope this book will contribute to that conversation.

Iain MacDonald, Inverness 2017

'The Board Must Have Powers to Act at Its Own Hand'

James Hunter

The Scottish government's decision to make Highlands and Islands Enterprise (HIE) responsible to an all-Scotland board, argues James Hunter, is the culmination of a series of moves to rein in, and now end, the independence of the north of Scotland's development agency. If permitted to stand, maintains Hunter, a historian as well as a former chair of HIE, this decision will signal the abandonment of a long-enduring and well-founded recognition that the Highlands and Islands are best served by institutions with the freedom to devise their own locally-formulated approaches to the particular needs of this most distinctive area.

My late mother, who grew up on a Kingairloch farm in the years immediately after World War One, remembered three annual highlights in the life of this small (and perhaps less than buzzing) community on the western side of Loch Linnhe. There was the day of Oban's Highland Games when, with luck, there would be an organised excursion to that North Argyll metropolis. There was New Year's Day. And there was the day – no less exciting than the other two in a small child's estimation – when a Board Bull was walked into Kingairloch by way of the hill road from Strontian.

This animal, as its title indicates, was the property of the Board of Agriculture for Scotland, a taxpayer-funded organisation whose principal task (outweighing its wider responsibilities) was to improve prospects for hard-pressed crofting and farming localities across the Highlands and Islands. Hence the substantial sums the Board of Agriculture spent on acquiring the thousands of acres on which its staff laid out, and helped equip, hundreds of new crofts. Hence, too, the board's livestock-improvement schemes – schemes geared to providing small-scale agriculturalists with higher quality breeding stock (like the bull recollected by my mother) than they would otherwise have been able to access.

As evidenced not just by my mother but also by plenty others in her age group, state-sponsored effort of this kind touched the lives of families from Kintyre to Shetland, from Strathspey to South Uist. So did the work of further public agencies that were to impact still more extensively on people living in Kingairloch and places like it: one of those places being Duror, on Loch Linnhe's other shore, where I myself was raised.

One of my earliest Duror memories is of the evening, not far into the 1950s, when my sister and I were able to greet our father's getting home from work by throwing the switch that, for the first time and miraculously as it seemed to us, filled our kitchen with what, for ages, we called 'electric light'.

Our ensuing relegation of Tilley lamps and candles to an understairs cupboard came about courtesy of the then ten-year-old North of Scotland Hydro-Electric Board which, under the formidable chairmanship of Tom Johnston, previously Secretary of State for Scotland in Winston Churchill's wartime coalition, defied Whitehall calls to concentrate on exporting hydro-electricity southwards, and insisted instead on connecting (at nominal cost) virtually every home in the Highlands and Islands to the national grid.

There would come a time in Britain's national politics – starting in Margaret Thatcher's 1980s heyday – when state-owned or state-financed institutions of every type came to be regarded with hostility. Perhaps this made some sort of sense to folk whose dealings with such institutions were mostly of the kind whereby hard-earned cash was shelled out for indifferent service from infamously unresponsive outfits like Post Office Telephones. But the numerous Highlands and Islands families whose crofts had been created by one public agency, or whose mains electricity had been provided by another, were never likely to embrace the belief that state intervention in national or regional economies is automatically to be deplored. Much the same is true of beneficiaries of the Highlands and Islands Development Board (HIDB), brought into existence when I was in secondary school in Oban, or the HIDB's successor agency, Highlands and Islands Enterprise (HIE), dating from 1991.

Because HIDB/HIE representatives have for decades been criss-crossing the Highlands and Islands, they have met with, and often lent a hand to, an enormous variety of people. HIDB/HIE personnel have dealt with the world's oil majors and with crofters; with globally-significant pharmaceutical firms and with fishermen, fish-farmers and foresters; and with hoteliers, restaurateurs and bed-and-breakfast operators. Some HIDB/HIE clients have had very large workforces. More have been one-person businesses. Others include the thousands of folk who have come in contact with the HIDB or HIE because they live in one of very many communities helped to construct or repair village halls; to establish museums, galleries, performance spaces, visitor attractions; to construct their own locally-controlled wind farms; *or* to purchase, and to develop, land, buildings and other assets. The one thing the HIDB and HIE have never been is invisible.

At times, to be sure, their high profile has led to the HIDB and HIE attracting as many brickbats as bouquets. As a journalist in the later 1970s and early 1980s, I made a modest living from articles that were condemnatory of what the HIDB was doing – or not doing – in relation to this, that or some other aspect of Highlands and Islands life. Nor have grounds for similar criticism been lacking more recently. As HIE chair between

1998 and 2004, I took comfort on occasion from the thought that a development agency which does not have failures is not taking enough risks – a less than wholly convincing justification, I admit, for having backed (with taxpayer cash) ventures which went awry.

But for all that it has long been easy to list HIDB/HIE disasters – a short-lived spectacle-frame factory in Barra and a transient tulip-growing scheme in the Uists were favoured targets in the early days – this has seldom been a prelude, in the Highlands and Islands anyway, to demanding drastic reductions (such as the one now on the cards) in HIDB/HIE status.

Hence an unforgettable comment made when the then Highland Regional Council discussed the possibility of the HIDB falling victim to a Thatcherite cull of public bodies. The HIDB, one councillor said, was as irresponsible as it was spendthrift. Far too many of its projects had folded. All that the HIDB had done was waste public money. 'But thank God', this councillor concluded, 'that the money's being wasted here.'

There is a just discernible echo there of remarks made by Kwame Nkrumah, the African nationalist who, in the 1950s, presided over Ghana's emergence from British colonial rule. Responding to jibes that Ghanaians were ill-equipped to take charge of their country's destiny, Nkrumah acknowledged that he and his colleagues would get things wrong. 'But the mistakes we make will be our own mistakes', he said, 'and it will be our responsibility to put them right.'

This argument – that only by having charge of their own affairs can people be made accountable for how those affairs are handled – is basic to the case for national self-determination. That is why Nkrumah-style remarks have been made over and over again by Scottish National Party (SNP) politicians looking to convince Scots to opt for independence. It is more than a bit ironic, then, that Scotland's devolved government, under SNP control since 2007, should itself be presiding over the eradication of what remains (after a now decade-long centralising drive) of HIE's capacity to frame its developmental strategies and its spending plans from a Highlands and Islands base and in light of Highlands and Islands requirements. Self-determination is regarded by SNP ministers as a very good thing in the context of their acquiring powers from London. But there is, it appears, to be no equivalent transfer of powers from Edinburgh to other parts of Scotland. Rather the reverse.

From a Highlands and Islands perspective, therefore, it is encouraging that – irrespective of such errors as it may have made – HIE continues to be viewed positively by the many individuals and groupings across the north who have made known (by way of press campaigns and public statements) that they want the agency, as the *Press and Journal* has put it repeatedly, 'kept local'.

The extent and force of this sentiment, I am told, has taken Scottish government policy-makers by surprise. 'It probably didn't occur to civil servants or ministers in Edinburgh', says Highlands MSP John Finnie of the Green Party, 'that a public agency like HIE might be viewed with respect, even affection, in the communities it serves.' Of itself, unfortunately, this strength of feeling will not ensure that SNP ministers backtrack. But it shows why they should.

The Highland Problem

The HIDB was set up with a view to its solving what had come to be called the Highland Problem. That problem was longstanding, its orgins bound up with upheavals set in train many years previously when large-scale sheep farming took the place of older land uses like cattle-rearing. Mass evictions or clearances (stemming from a need to give incoming sheep farmers sole occupancy of whole tracts of territory) were followed by the beginnings of a Highlands and Islands population exodus. Family after family left in search of the better prospects thought (rightly) to be available elsewhere in the United Kingdom or (still more) in overseas countries and colonies like the United States, Canada and Australia.

Emigration was not universally affordable. Poorer people were dumped, after their eviction, on miniscule crofts where only one crop, potatoes, could be grown in sufficient quantity to keep families in food for twelve months out of twelve. In the later 1840s when successive potato harvests were everywhere wiped out by blight, the unavoidable outcome was famine. Given that the Highlands and Islands, together with still more stricken Ireland, were components of what was then the world's most successful country, it can seem extraordinary in retrospect that so dreadful a situation could have arisen. This, however, was a time when British governments were in thrall to theorising that forbade interference with, or regulation of, market economies – even when the upshot was humanitarian catastrophe. Just as it was not for politicians to stop a landlord making hundreds of families homeless, neither was it for those same politicians to grapple with the causes of poverty and hunger.

Doctrines of this kind have life in them still – both in Britain and further afield. But in the Highlands and Islands they were nevertheless challenged, with enduring consequences, in the 1880s when crofters at last rebelled against treatment they had long been expected to endure in silence. Initially, the authorities responded to crofter-organised protests and rent-strikes by deploying the police and the military in a vain attempt to restore order. But then the Liberal prime minister of the time, William Gladstone, conceded that crofting grievances were well-founded. Hence the Crofters Act of 1886.

This milestone legislation made renewed clearance impossible by granting crofters security of tenure. It also put in place a judicial tribunal tasked with fixing fair rents and otherwise advancing crofting interests. Those measures ensured the continuation of crofting. More fundamentally, they established the principle that the Highlands and Islands could and should be seen as a distinctive area meriting, first, its own unique policy prescriptions and, second, the setting up of such institutions as might be needed to put those prescriptions into effect.

It is this principle, one that has served the Highlands and Islands well for more than 100 years, that is being undermined and endangered by the centralising obsessions of the present Scottish government and, not least, by this government's apparent determination to turn HIE into little more than a means of implementing policy decisions taken outside the Highlands and Islands by people with next to no Highland and Islands involvements. The eventual outcome, if the current administration in Holyrood continues down the path it has of late been following, will be to restore pre-1886 arrangements – arrangements predicated on the assumption that the Highlands and Islands ought to be treated, economically, developmentally and in other ways, on the same basis as the rest of Scotland. No longer, in those circumstances, will there be scope for Highlands and Islands initiatives of the kind promoted or endorsed, over a lengthy period, by a succession of UK and Scottish politicians.

Several such initatives were listed in March 1965 when, in a powerful and often emotional speech, Willie Ross, Secretary of State for Scotland in Harold Wilson's then recently-elected Labour government, introduced in the House of Commons the legislation that created the Highlands and Islands Development Board.

'There is no part of those islands of ours that has merited or received more attention from this House', Ross told MPs, 'than the Highlands and Islands.' From the 1880s forward, Liberal, Conservative and Labour ministers had accepted that conditions in the north of Scotland were such as to warrant a series of regionally specific measures. That was why the Highlands and Islands had acquired their own land laws; why new crofts had been created on a wholesale basis; why, as far back as the 1890s, the then privately-owned railway network had been extended to Mallaig and Kyle of Lochalsh at public expense; why generous sums had been invested in new roads, bridges and piers; why a Highlands and Islands Medical Service (a localised precursor of the later NHS) had been launched in 1913; and why the Hydro Board had been allowed, and eventually encouraged, to make electricity supplies available to community after community, island after island.

Cumulatively, Willie Ross said, the effect had been to ensure that life in the Highlands and Islands was 'a bit better than it was'. To that extent, the numerous north of Scotland policy programmes brought before the House of Commons had 'met with some success'. But they had 'never really succeeded', Ross observed, 'in stemming the depopulation of the Highlands and Islands'. And because continuing population loss was recognised to be the most obvious (as well as the most debilitating) manifestation of the Highland Problem, it was clear that yet more action was required.

Very Great Powers

During the famine years of the 1840s, the population of the Highlands and Islands – in marked contrast to the breakneck expansion then occurring both in Lowland Scotland and in much of England – began to fall. That fall continued, decade after decade, into the mid-20th century when, between 1931 and 1951, the number of people in some localities shrank by as much as a fifth or a quarter.

In response, *Picture Post*, then the UK's most widely read magazine, sent one of its staffers to the Highlands and Islands. The region's 'dwindling communities', this journalist commented, were symptomatic of the Highlands and Islands having become 'Britain's most gravely depressed area'. A confidential report prepared for government was equally gloomy: 'In brief, the Highland scene presents a picture of [an outward] drift ... leaving behind a diminished and ageing population which, in many of the remoter sectors, is approaching a position at which it can no longer maintain itself.'

The 1950s and early 1960s were a period when British voters, benefiting from a nationally thriving economy, were told by their prime minister that 'they had never had it so good'. But from this boom the north of Scotland stood apart. By me and by most of my Oban High School classmates, and by our parents also, it was taken for granted that, if we wanted to get on in life, we would begin by heading elsewhere. Three or four good 'Highers' and a student grant were our equivalents of the emigrant ships that had taken our 19th-century counterparts across the Atlantic Ocean. 'For every [Highlands and Islands] child', Willie Ross informed MPs in 1965, 'a School Leaving Certificate is a visa for the south, and the road past the croft too often has been the road for a one-way traffic out.'

If the loss of people from the north was to be halted and reversed, Ross continued, it would no longer be sufficient to respond to the region's difficulties on a piecemeal basis. 'It has become more and more obvious to everyone who studies the [Highlands and Islands]', he said, 'that ... what really has been needed is an authority with executive powers to deal comprehensively with problems; not to deal with them one at a time but comprehensively. For this reason we have decided to establish [a] ... Development Board.'

'For 200 years', the Secretary of State declared, 'the Highlander has been the man on Scotland's conscience ... No part of Scotland has been given a shabbier deal by history.' For far too long there had been 'only one way out of his troubles for the person born in the Highlands – emigration'. That this was so was a reproach to the wider society of which the Highlands and Islands were part. 'No country can claim happiness if one of its most splendid assets – in this case its unsurpassed landscape – can be enjoyed only in the dreams of exiles.' It was in no way surprising, therefore, that the provisions of the government's Highlands and Islands Development Bill had been 'seized on' with 'avidity' in Scotland: 'It is high time', most commentators seemed to imply, 'that a serious step was taken to redress history in this respect.'

The Labour government, Ross went on, was prepared to invest heavily in Highlands and Islands development. 'But do not let us pretend', he warned, 'that all that needs to be done … is to wave a golden wand and all will be well. We have to be realistic about this. The [Development] Board will have no easy task. Imagination, patience and persistence will be needed.'

Above all, or so the Secretary of State contended, the soon-to-be-established HIDB had to have sole charge of assessing what needed doing in the Highlands and Islands – as well as the freedom to get on with doing it by whatever means were thought appropriate. 'The board', Willie Ross insisted, 'must have powers to act at its own hand.' Hence the wide remit embodied in the HIDB's founding legislation. 'For the purpose of assisting the people of the Highlands and Islands to improve their economic and social conditions and of enabling the Highlands and Islands to play a more effective part in the economic and social development of the nation', the eventual Act laid down, 'there shall be established a Highlands and Islands Development Board which shall have the general function of preparing, concerting, promoting, assisting and undertaking measures for the economic and social development of the Highlands and Islands.'

This was revolutionary. Elsewhere in the UK, and for that matter internationally, development agencies were, and are, thought to have largely or exclusively *economic* purposes – the Scottish Development Agency (SDA), established in 1975 and now Scottish Enterprise (SE), being typical in this regard. But because the HIDB was seen from the first to have *social* as well as economic responsibilities, and because those responsibilities were transferred to HIE when that organisation took over the HIDB's role in 1991, both the HIDB and HIE have engaged with the Highlands and Islands on a much broader front than more conventional such agencies could have done. Like the SDA or SE, the HIDB and HIE have made grants and loans – sometimes large grants and loans – to both established and incoming businesses and industries. Unlike their rest-of-Scotland counterparts, however, the HIDB and HIE have also engaged directly with individuals, families and community groups in ways of the sort already illustrated.

The exceptional nature of what he called the 'very great powers' bestowed on himself and his colleagues by the Highlands and Islands Development Act of 1965 was instantly apparent to the HIDB's first chairman, Robert Grieve. It was this, Grieve commented in his foreword to the HIDB's first annual report, that had led to there being 'world interest' in what was seen to be a globally significant 'experiment in regional development'. It is this experiment that today's Scottish government is bringing to an end.

Little Short Of Astonishing

Had the approach embarked on in 1965 failed conspicuously to deliver positive results, there would be some justification for the Scottish government's assault on HIDB/HIE's founding principles – principles embodied in the autonomy SNP ministers are taking away. The reverse, however, is the case. This is highlighted by one remarkable statistic. In the 51 years since the HIDB took shape, the population of the area now served by HIE has increased by nearly 100,000, or more than 22 per cent.

This rate of increase, as stressed subsequently, has been by no means experienced universally across the Highlands and Islands.

But that does not detract from the significance of the figures just cited. From the 1840s to the 1960s, despite all the good work done by organisations as diverse as the Board of Agriculture and the Hydro Board, the number of people living in the Highlands and Islands *as a whole* was on a steady, sometimes precipitous, downward trajectory. Since the later 1960s, the opposite has been true.

The truly startling nature of this reversal is apparent from two further points. First, the post-1965 rate of population growth in the Highlands and Islands has been much higher than that of Scotland generally – the all-Scotland rate, during the same period, being just 2 per cent. Second, the Highlands and Islands record (underlined by the area's population increase being equivalent to four-fifths of Scotland's post-1960s population gain) is little short of astonishing in light of the fact that, prior to this period, the region was synonymous – as Willie Ross emphasised in 1965 – with runaway out-migration.

Not all of this turnaround is down to HIDB/HIE. But a lot of it is. And basic to this HIDB/HIE achievement are the very attributes the Scottish government is intent on removing – most notably the agency's now-threatened freedom to act in accordance with objectives determined by its own independent board.

There have been, as already acknowledged, plenty of mistakes and mis-steps along the way. To begin with, for instance, the HIDB was reluctant to exploit the full breadth of its remit. Although Willie Ross had contended that 'land is the basic natural resource of the Highlands and Islands and any plan … for development would be meaningless if proper use of land were not a part of it', the HIDB refused to challenge a land ownership structure that (quite apart from any other consideration) was responsible for a good deal of the population loss the new organisation had been set up to make good. Nor was the small business sector the priority it afterwards became.

The HIDB preferred initially to concentrate, by way of several projected 'growth centres', on the depopulation-defeating potential of incoming, and ideally large-scale, industry.

To development agencies, as to politicians, the attractions of this sort of proceeding are understandable. When, in 2010 and 2011, SE and the Scottish government made millions available to Amazon with a view to persuading that company to establish a distribution centre in Fife, hundreds of jobs were promptly magicked into existence. This, from an SE and government standpoint, outweighed criticism to the effect that those jobs are (arguably) of poor quality and that it is (just as arguably) indefensible to be shovelling public money in the direction of a vastly profitable multinational corporation which pays almost no UK tax on its immense UK turnover. Politically, then, it can make sense to prefer immediate gains in Amazon-type jobs (however badly paid) to the necessarily longer-term, and far more challenging, task of encouraging indigenous enterprise.

So it was with the 1960s HIDB. 'It would be daft', one of the organisation's board members remarked, 'to try and catch sprats when they could catch a whale.' Elsewhere in the British public sector, as it happens, the economist E. F. Schumacher was then working up ideas he would shortly encapsulate in a highly influential book entitled *Small is Beautiful*. Nothing was more counter-productive developmentally, Schumacher argued, than what he called 'the idolatry of gigantism'. But this, at the outset, was an idolatry the HIDB found hard to set aside.

That changed. It did so in part as a result of the HIDB hiring Robert Storey. When, in the 1980s, the HIDB's then chair, Bob Cowan, commented that the board had been 'lucky to employ many lively and energetic people [who] ... do not conform to the popular stereotype of the public service employee', he is bound to have had Storey (among others) in mind.

Back in the 1950s, Shetland's county council, grappling in those post-War years with economic collapse, had made Storey its development officer. In this role he contributed enormously to a regenerative effort which (by the mid-1960s and well in advance of offshore oil's arrival on the scene) had brought full employment, and the beginnings of repopulation, to Shetland. This was accomplished, Storey maintained, by overturning both external and internal perceptions of the island group and its inhabitants – not least by getting folk to think positively about what had previously seemed entirely negative. 'The isolation that had so far bedevilled them in the twentieth century', Bob Storey said of the islands where he began his career, 'could perhaps be a virtue and a strength. Isolation made for the integration of the community and a stronger identity. The fact that Shetland was undeniably Shetland, and Shetlanders were so undeniably what they were, could perhaps be their greatest strength in this matter of development.' Thinking of that kind, when applied to the wider Highlands and Islands, would be a key contributor to the renaissance (of which regional-level population growth is just one indicator) which HIDB and HIE have done much to bring about.

The Enterprise and Skills Review which preceded the decision to subject HIE to external control has nothing to say about such matters in a somewhat jargon-laden report that, though its authors aspire 'to maximise economic opportunity in all parts of the country', concludes that 'the optimal fit between national and local priorities' will best be brought about by putting a whole range of diverse organisations – HIE, SE, the Scottish Funding Council (responsible for higher education finance) and a still undefined South of Scotland development agency – 'under the direction of a single board'.

By such means, or so it is insisted by the responsible minister, Keith Brown, the Scottish government will attain its 'ambition … for Scotland to rank among the top performing OECD nations'. That aim is nothing if not laudable. But it is hard to believe (given the extent to which successful development depends on sensitivity to local complexities) that it will be accomplished by means of still more centralisation of what the Scottish government and its advisers call 'the enterprise and skills support system'.

Take, for example, Scotland's need (one made much of by the Enterprise and Skills Review) to foster business innovation: in a word, entrepreneurialism. Nothing being perfect in this world, entrepreneurial drive and ambition could doubtless be backed more effectively than they have been by our 'support system'. But it takes more than such backing to engender and nurture entrepreneurialism where social and other circumstances have long precluded its emergence. In these circumstances, developmental effort has to start at a far more basic level. That, perhaps, is the key finding to emerge from the 'experiment in regional development' the HIDB and HIE have been presiding over in the north.

Still Uncompleted

Starting a long time ago, generation after generation in the Highlands and Islands were told by most folk in authority that practically everything about them and the places where they lived was of little or no value. Their Gaelic language, like their Shetlandic and other dialects, were described as second-rate, inferior and backward. Their home districts, it was said, were bereft of resources, geographically peripheral and, it followed, incapable of catching up with, let alone surpassing, more fortunately placed localities. That the Highlands and Islands were viewed in this light by outsiders was bad enough. That the region came, in time, to be regarded in much the same way by its own residents was worse. When personal betterment was something that could only be accomplished elsewhere – a prevalent notion in the Highlands into which I was born – economic contraction and depopulation became both inescapable and self-reinforcing.

That is why the still-uncompleted regeneration of the Highlands and Islands had to commence with restoring our formerly demoralised population's sense of worth; with encouraging both individuals and communities to take pride in their background; with making people feel good about themselves and their surroundings; with showing that the Highlands and Islands, so long dismissed as hopelessly impoverished, are actually rich in music, architecture, literature, archaeology and much else; with insisting that the Highlands and Islands, so well endowed culturally, are even wealthier environmentally; and with demonstrating that our outstanding heritage, both natural and human, can offer all our people, whether established residents or newcomers, an exceptionally high quality of life.

Hence HIDB/HIE commitment (a commitment dating from Bob Storey's time) to backing all sorts of undertakings that, on the face of things, have little to do with economic development as commonly understood: local history societies; heritage centres; theatres; the *Fèisean* movement which has brought about a flowering of interest in traditional music and song; Gaelic-medium playgroups; Scotland's Gaelic-medium college at Sabhal Mòr Ostaig in Skye; football clubs; and sports and leisure facilities. Investments of this kind (and there have been a lot of them) were made not because HIDB/HIE considered that enhancing the standing of, say, Gaelic or traditional music is good in itself – though it is. What has underpinned all such spending is a conviction that to do this sort of thing is simultaneously to boost self-belief and self-confidence in ways that eventually translate into increased business activity.

In a publication marking the 50th anniversary of the HIDB's formation, author Catherine Deveney told how she visited Skye to meet Campbell Grant, managing director of Sitekit Ltd, a software company launched on the island in 1989 and still headquartered there though now operating internationally. By Campbell's parents' generation, Deveney reported, both Skye and Gaelic were considered dead ends. 'But now', Deveney wrote, 'his children speak the language of their grandparents ... Times have changed.'

'Campbell has another visitor when I call,' Deveney went on. 'Malcolm Henry, his close friend since schooldays, has dropped by for a chat ... They have both run businesses on the island and have seen confidence in the area grow. "We were part of the first generation who were not just trying to get away," says Campbell. "If you had any ambition, you weren't meant to stay here," agrees Malcolm. But, says Campbell, "The HIDB helped change that attitude."'

This exchange is illustrative of the developmental outcomes of HIDB/HIE willingness to take measures that might not deliver employment dividends for decades. Will such measures be high on the agenda of what the Scottish government call an 'overarching board' that will one moment be dealing with the revenue requirements of Edinburgh University, the next with mega-investments of the Amazon sort and, a few minutes later, with the needs of Borders towns like Hawick and Jedburgh? Maybe. But many folk in the north think – with good reason – that decision-makers located far away (and dealing with what looks like a crazily mixed portfolio of responsibilities) are unlikely to have anything approximating to HIE's painfully acquired understanding of what it takes to bring better times to badly run-down Highlands and Islands neighbourhoods.

Those worries are common to both community activists and business representatives. There is 'a widely-shared concern' among his members in the north, the Scottish Council for Development and Industry's Inverness-based director has commented, that the Scottish government's treatment of HIE 'risks diminishing an organisation which has, over the long-term, played a pivotal role in driving the kind of step-change in economic prosperity we have seen'.

The Enterprise and Skills Review's response is that the Scottish government will 'maintain dedicated support' for HIE by continuing the organisation's operational activities on the ground. But that, in relation to points made here, offers scant reassurance. HIE, when answering always to external authority, will be wholly incapable of launching the sometimes buccaneering projects that have been characteristic of HIDB/ HIE at its best. Only independent boards and their chairs can do that.

When, in the 1980s and 1990s, first HIDB and then HIE spent heavily on ISDN (Integrated Services Digital Network) provision with a view to putting the Highlands and Islands at the forefront of the then barely-started communications revolution that led eventually to the worldwide web, there was much grumbling that the cash involved was being squandered. In the event, this spending, with which HIDB and HIE boards persisted in the face of all such condemnation, made possible the emergence of companies like Campbell Grant's Sitekit – as well as paving the way for the now near-universal adoption by Highlands and Islands companies of internet-based marketing strategies that go a long way to overcoming once insurmountable barriers of distance between them and potential customers.

Will a board with a Scotland-wide role place the Highlands and Islands at the front of the queue for analogous outlays in future? Hardly. Even more improbable is the likelihood of such a board doing as Bob Cowan did when, with strong support from then Highland Regional Council education committee convener Val MacIver, he threw his weight behind the concept of a University of the Highlands and Islands (UHI). Cowan's stance, backed with a great deal of HIDB/HIE money, was one that senior civil servants viewed with undisguised scepticism – not to say hostility. Since just such civil servants (inherently hyper-cautious in outlook) will exercise much influence on the Scottish government's planned 'overarching board', there would have been little chance, had such an entity been in charge of Highlands and Islands development in the past, of UHI (now a vital contributor to north betterment) having come into existence.

Not Like Norway

Comprehensive accounts and analyses of HIDB/HIE achievements have never been attempted, and certainly not by the authors of the Scottish government's Enterprise and Skills Review. But here (in summary form, in no particular order, and in addition to topics touched on already) are a number of Highlands and Islands developments to which the HIDB, HIE or both have made substantial, often decisive, contributions:

- Since the 1970s, and for the first time in centuries, more people have been moving into the Highlands and Islands than have been moving out – many of those new arrivals bringing with them valuable skills, capital and expertise.
- Tourism continues to expand across the north, its growth boosted by a proliferation of first-rate restaurants and eating places making more and more creative use of local produce.
- Despite there being many more people here than formerly, the Highlands and Islands unemployment rate, once a multiple of the Scottish average, has for a long time been below the all-Scotland figure.
- Since the 1990s, more than half a million acres have been brought into community ownership. Locally-formed land trusts (their emergence facilitated and assisted in virtually every case by HIE) everywhere demonstrate that homes can be built, population increased, businesses created and

loss-making estates brought into profit in places where those things were formerly thought impossible.

- The rate of business start-ups in the Highlands and Islands has, for years now, been above the rate in Scotland as a whole.

- Cutting-edge ventures include the Highland Diabetes Institute in Inverness's (HIE-aided) Centre for Health Science and the (again HIE-aided) European Marine Energy Centre (EMEC) in Orkney – where HIE and Orkney Islands Council are presently building on EMEC's success by jointly creating a £7 million Renewables Research and Innovation Campus.

- Not least because of advances of this sort, and as shown by recent surveys, more than half of our young people think that the Highlands and Islands have, in recent years, become a better place.

- As demonstrated by the same surveys, young people who choose to stay in the Highlands and Islands (the sort of people often categorised as failures in the past) are today regarded positively both by their elders and by their own age-group. Six out of ten such 'stayers' say that they are here because they value their locality's quality of life.

- As that last finding indicates, young people in the Highlands and Islands are proud of where they live, with some 80 per cent believing themselves fortunate to be associated with their home town or community.

- Across the Highlands and Islands there has been an explosion of arts, book and music festivals of almost every kind.

- Since the mid-1960s, the economic activity rate (which measures overall income-earning involvements) in the Highlands and Islands has increased from around 80 per cent of the Scottish average to more than 100 per cent of that average.

There is, then, no shortage of reasons as to why the Scottish government should be reinforcing HIE's capacity to get good things done. Instead, the SNP administrations in power since 2007 have sought consistently to circumscribe HIE's freedom of action and to limit financial and other support of the sort previously available to the agency – whether from the Scottish Office prior to the creation of a Scottish Parliament or from Holyrood thereafter.

An early straw in the wind was the incoming SNP government's prompt ending of its predecessor administration's public sector jobs dispersal programme, which HIE backed strongly and which resulted, among other gains, in the transfer of Scottish Natural Heritage's headquarters from Edinburgh to Inverness. Henceforth, as the axing of the jobs dispersal initiative indicated, centralisation, not decentralising, was to be the order of the day. Responsibility for management of European Union (EU) development funding in the north was duly transferred from a north-focused consortium of HIE, local authorities and other Highlands and Islands interests to Holyrood ministers. Where strategic controls of any consequence had been assigned to the Highlands and Islands, it was now apparent, those controls were to be resumed by government.

In accordance with this new approach, SNP ministers abolished HIE's ten Local Enterprise Companies (LECs). That generated little in the way of cash savings, LEC chairs and board members having been unpaid. It did serve, however, to deprive island groups and mainland districts like Shetland, the Western Isles, Moray, Ross-shire and Lochaber of what had previously been a valuable stake in policy-making. Nor were LEC policy-formulation functions, on their being lost to places like Lerwick or Stornoway, entrusted to HIE's head office in Inverness. Shorn of its LECs and with its budget cut, HIE, it emerged, was henceforth to be treated as a Scottish government 'delivery agency' – the organisation, in consequence, no longer having the 'powers to act at its own hand' that a Labour Secretary of State had granted to the HIDB and that Conservative Secretaries of State (when, in the late 1980s, they decided to replace the HIDB with a new body) made available to HIE.

All of this is of a piece with SNP ministers' apparent wish to replicate in Scotland one of the wider United Kingdom's least desirable features. Just as political, financial and other power has been overly concentrated in London – to the great detriment of the English North and Midlands – so power north of the border, it seems, is similarly to be concentrated in Edinburgh.

Rhetorically, much is made in SNP circles of what Scotland might learn from Norway. But far from seeking to replicate that country's enviably dispersed governance structures, SNP ministers – not just in relation to HIE but in relation to the police, local government and much else – have aspired, for the most part, to be in sole charge of how Scotland is run. It is as if the Holyrood machine, despite (or perhaps because of) the governing party's electoral dominance, is unwilling to concede the possibility that it might not be Scotland's one and only source of wisdom.

Like SNP ministers, I want Scotland to be an independent country. That is why I am an SNP voter and party member. Unlike SNP ministers, however, I am firmly of the view that Scotland (a small but diverse nation where the North-east, the Borders, the South-west and other areas are, in their own ways, just as unique as the Highlands and Islands) is not well served by centralism and control-freakery of the sort that have become of late so all-pervasive.

Which is not to say that an agency like HIE should forever be immune from scrutiny and reform. The HIDB and HIE, to repeat, have had their failings. Of these, the most significant was foreshadowed in a paper Robert Grieve presented to colleagues within six months of the HIDB coming into existence. 'No matter what success is achieved in the eastern or central Highlands', Grieve wrote in March 1966, 'the board will be judged by its ability to hold population in the true crofting areas.' The HIDB/HIE record, in this respect, is best examined in the light of 1961-2011 census data from the eight 'sub-areas' into which HIE, for reporting and other purposes, presently divides the Highlands and Islands.

Collectively, as highlighted earlier, those localities experienced a 1961-2011 population increase of 22 per cent. But separately their performances varied hugely. In three sub-areas overall growth was exceeded. These were: the Inner Moray Firth (including Inverness and Easter Ross) where the 50-year growth rate was 71 per cent; Lochaber, Skye and Wester Ross where the rate was 36 per cent; and Shetland where it was 30 per cent.

Two areas, while recording increases, came in below the regional average. These were Moray at 18 per cent and Orkney at 14 per cent. Three further areas, however, experienced population falls in the half-century from 1961. These were Caithness and Sutherland where the loss was in the order of 3 per cent; mainland Argyll and its neighbouring islands where it was 6 per cent; and the Western Isles where population fell by 15 per cent.

Some comfort can perhaps be taken from the most recent inter-census decade, 2001-2011, when only one HIE sub-area, Argyll, lost population – at a ten-year rate of 2 per cent. But this in no way serves to blunt the wider point that, in much of the Highlands and Islands, there is still a big developmental job to be completed.

In what Robert Grieve called 'the true crofting areas' that job has been tackled most impressively in Skye. There, before famine struck in the 1840s, population was in the order of 25,000. By the mid-1960s, when the HIDB took shape, the corresponding figure was under 7,000. Had that rate of decline persisted, Skye today would (theoretically) be home to nobody. In fact, population loss has been reversed spectacularly – the island's present population of above 10,000 representing a net gain of around 50 per cent.

But if Skye (not just in the vicinity of its main settlement, Portree, but in truly rural Sleat in the south of the island) is today awash with new homes, and if there are more modest signs of demographic and economic turnaround in other communities in the Hebrides and on the west coast mainland, it nevertheless remains the case that there are plenty of places in the Highlands and Islands that are not yet participating fully (or at all) in the upturn that has indubitably occurred in the rest of the region.

Among them (and this list is by no means exhaustive) are: Argyll and Bute towns like Rothesay and Dunoon; Argyll islands like Islay, Jura and Colonsay; the Western Isles; north-west Sutherland; Caithness (where the closure of the Dounreay nuclear facility has had a most debilitating effect); and more outlying islands in both Orkney and Shetland. It is on localities like these, or so an informed review of HIE might conclude, that the agency needs in future to concentrate.

Would such a review – if conducted by people with some understanding of how the Highlands and Islands came to be the way they are – advise that a board located in the Scottish Central Belt (and with all sorts of Central Belt issues before it) would be better placed to deal imaginatively with the difficulties confronting, say, Durness or Lewis than an equivalent grouping situated in the Highlands and Islands? That seems improbable. It seems especially improbable in light of the HIDB/HIE story told here.

If the lessons of that story were to be acted on, the Scottish government would today be considering entirely different proposals as to how HIE could best be revamped. Among such proposals, surely, would be a recommendation to the effect that the HIE board should not just be kept in being but should at once be re-empowered with a view to restoring to HIE the strategic roles already filched from it by SNP ministers.

Nor is the HIDB/HIE experience, or so a full-scale appraisal of that experience might conclude, without relevance for the rest of Scotland. If there is to be a development agency dealing with areas like Dumfries and Galloway – more disadvantaged today than a substantial slice of the Highlands and Islands – then that agency, too, ought arguably to have far-reaching capabilities (social as well as economic) of the kind the HIDB acquired in 1965.

And what of urban Scotland? The Highlander, Willie Ross told the House of Commons, was the man on Scotland's conscience. Today, the person on our nation's conscience ought indisputably to be the child, woman or man condemned (by residence in one of our written-off housing schemes) to have many fewer life chances and, on average, a markedly shorter life than the rest of us. In what is by global standards a rich country, this is an inexcusable state of affairs. It is one that needs putting right with commitment and resolve of the kind that brought so many benefits when, half a century ago, the causes of the Highland Problem began at last to be urgently addressed.

'The efforts of this Board will have world significance'

Robert Grieve

Professor Robert Grieve was the first chairman of the Highlands and Islands Development Board, appointed by a Labour government. A career civil servant, he described his own career as 'falling up the ladder'. Qualified as a civil engineer, he was involved in the post-War planning for the Clyde Valley that helped shape the modern Glasgow before taking up his new job in the north in his fifties. One newspaper announced his appointment under the headline 'Grieve for Scotland', but the Highlands and Islands were to have many reasons to rejoice at his appointment. On the next few pages, we publish extracts of his first ever annual report as chairman of the HIDB.

First Report (1st November 1965 to 31st December 1966)

Presented to Parliament in pursuance of Section 3 (le) of the Highlands and Islands Development (Scotland) Act, 1965

Foreword

1. The Scot easily falls into a belief that he and his attitudes are of world interest. He certainly has a world image, some facets of which are truly admirable but a great number of which are either romantic or out of date to the point of standing in the path of his true progress.

2. It is therefore easy to flatter ourselves that an experiment in regional development such as the Board is carrying out is

of world interest. However, such a statement is absolutely and strictly true.

3. It is essential that we should realise this, all of us in Britain, and recognise that the Board is setting out to do a job now recognised as one of the important preoccupations of government in western civilisation. The job is to tackle the areas of their countries that the various revolutions in agriculture, industry and technology have passed by. In all cases, almost everywhere that one can think of, these countries wish to "develop" such areas but, at the same time, have strong emotional feelings about a way of life in them which has its virtues and values, dimly seen to be necessary ingredients in any healthy society.

4. Whether the areas, as in the United States, are called "poverty areas"; whether, as in the south of Italy, with its Cassa per il Mezzogiorno, the problem affects a congested and poor people living in the conditions of the last century; whether, as in Norway and similar countries, the problem is of small numbers of people holding down, and keeping civilised, enormous areas of difficult territory; whether, as in Holland, it is the attempt to do "land consolidation" schemes to bring backward agricultural areas into a more productive arena of activity; whether, as in Eire, it is a country suffering from a kind of economic anaemia and making admirable efforts to give new life and purpose to its people; the effort and methods have a general similarity throughout. The Tennessee Valley Authority was a great inspiration to those people all over the world 30 years ago who believed in doing something vigorous and specific about these problems.

5. The Highlands and Islands Development Act gives very great powers to this Board; powers regarded as being concordant with the intractable character of the problems involved. These emerged from a general build-up of feeling about the need for something to be done in the Highlands and from a study of all these concurrent attempts being made in western civilisation

and elsewhere. It is therefore, as I say, no exaggeration to claim that the efforts of this Board will have world significance.

6. The Board is deeply aware of all this and recognises that a greater pride and tenacity, and some sense of nobility, may emerge from a realisation of this by the people of the Highlands; and that they may soon be leading the world in an exciting effort. Our Board has tried to express within itself a simple aim—the aim of adding another perfectly possible way of life to that in the great cities. In offering that alternative to the important minority in any urbanised country who wish to take it, the Board will also be engendering a greater flow of products for the United Kingdom.

7. That is the measure of our activity; that is the challenge which the Board has knowingly accepted.

The Challenge

8. The creation of the Board must be taken as evidence of a special problem requiring a special agency for its solution. From that it is clear that there has been dissatisfaction with past policies—although that by no means proves that all or even the majority of these policies were fundamentally wrong. Some may indeed have been wrong only in time or scale. The important thing is that general agreement seems to exist on the proposition that they did not solve the "Highland Problem".

9. If it were not clear to the Board before, it is very clear now after its first year that a substantial step forward towards a solution is quite possible if even a broad measure of agreement were visible on the elements of the "Highland Problem". But it is probably the measure of the problem that a host of definitions exist, are passionately pressed upon us, and are so often mutually exclusive. This is not to make a debating point—it is only too painfully and evidently true.

10. The Board has, in real fact, paid great attention to all points of view; has studied all the reports and papers that have been produced in such abundance over the decades; and has attempted to keep up-to-date with similar efforts in other parts of the world. A constant stream of information comes into us; we will engender more and we will seek new techniques of development wherever they are to be found, here or in any other country. Every member of the Board and many of the staff have been deeply interested in Highland affairs for a long time and have been involved in working on them in one way or another.

11. In the midst of such a complexity of opinion, some simple facts and aims must be the basis of understanding and the impetus for action. What are they?

12. It is significant that most opinions, as we have studied and listened to them, accept that depopulation of the area is the central problem—indeed, it is almost the only common factor. The only exception to that is a curiously diverse group of attitudes, almost wholly urban in origin, which sees the Highlands as the natural relief valve for an over-urbanised country—in fact, as a kind of "national wilderness". We have heard this opinion expressed frequently, although not often publicly, by influential and responsible people.

13. But this attitude would, if openly expressed, be rejected by the great majority of the Scottish people at least—and particularly by resident Highlanders. The difficulty of those, however, who wish to see the Highlands a thriving, populated area is in expressing some mutually acceptable attitude or solution to the problem of holding people in the Highlands.

Range of Solutions

14. The common range of solutions here extends from the extreme "Highland way of life" concept, which seems to mean

crofters of an idealised character exempt from the ordinary laws of making a real livelihood, to an admittedly more efficient, but fundamentally, agricultural economy with very small "light industries" here and there largely to justify the continuance of certain necessary and comforting services; and with forestry represented very largely by its capacity to shelter stock. In this context industry and tourism are accepted as necessary evils and forestry suspect either as (a) something which pre-empts land that should produce food or (b) a sinister monoculture that will blanket, before its inevitable ecological disaster, the beauty and variety of the "traditional" Highlands—forgetting that much of the bare and spectacular beauty of the Highlands is, in sober fact, a standing example of such a disaster.

15. The Board can see and appreciate all the historic, romantic, economic, preservationist, social and even music-hall influences that have produced this confusion of ideals and attitudes— but is aware of the vested interests, cultural, economic and sporting, that use the various elements of them as they suit their arguments. We are belaboured equally by those who say we should be taking over great areas of land and splitting them up into small farms; and by those who regard the crofting way of life as false, uneconomic, rotted by subsidies and leading to an inevitable, if euphoric, death.

16. We are pressed strongly by some areas to get on with tourism, and by others to abjure this threat to a "way of life". Here, as elsewhere, there is an implicit assumption that any manufacturing industry, no matter how useless or dubious its product in terms of sense, is somehow more honourable than an industry which is designed to give a visitor a warm welcome, a comfortable bed and good food.

17. This is, of course, a cartoon of a much more subtle amalgam of attitudes; the thing the Board wishes to express here is that there must be few areas in Britain which demonstrate so much

difficulty in presenting, and having roughly accepted, a common set of policies. We recognise elements of genuine concern and genuine truth in all the attitudes touched on but we suggest that public relations is not an easy problem within such a confusion of aims.

18. We know, and all should appreciate, that the Highlands and Islands are a huge area, one-fifth of Britain, one-half of Scotland, and it is no truckling to easy compromise to say that all of these attitudes can find real expression in such a vast and varied area. The Board, therefore, must take the lead here and declare a broad set of policies which, it believes, can meet the needs and desires of the country in general, the Highlander in particular and lead to an eventual solution of the Highland problem. We can express them simply and present them as the alignment along which our whole strategy is set. This point in time, after one year's work, must be the point where they are presented for discussion by all those concerned, and for our instruction and advice relevant to our future work.

19. We see, therefore, relevant weights and priorities something as follows:

20. **Agriculture**, which, it must be remembered, so often simply has meant sheep rearing in the Highlands, will, as it is practised at present, worsen the depopulation problem and also the problem of greater production. It must remain, however, an important part of the Highland economy. The Board believes that much more can be produced from the Highlands but is very clear that this is highly unlikely to be accompanied by an increasing population in these activities; rather is it likely to be accompanied by a drop because of more efficient and mechanised methods. The Board will back any move in the direction of more production and where, as in certain highly productive enterprises, it means also more jobs the Board will redouble its efforts to help. Here, therefore, the result would be

more food from the Highlands for the rest of the country rather than more people for the Highlands.

21. **Forestry** is of great importance and this is universally recognised. Indeed, its acreage in the Highlands must be extended, but more and more purposefully in its location relative to the transport and utilisation of the timber; and more carefully, bearing in mind the recreational and tourist value of the Highlands, in its effect on the appearance of landscape. Forestry is one of the three great hopes for rural employment and a more secure Highland economy; its excellent research work gives hope, too, for planting in areas hitherto regarded as impossible. Finally, and simply, we are a grossly under-forested country relative to most other comparable countries in the world.

22. **Tourism** is the second great prop available to us but unlike forestry, whose effects must necessarily be long-term, tourism can make a rapid impact on the economy of the Highlands and on the numbers of people that the area can support. Its potential is great but it must:

(a) be more selective in its planning and publicity for specialised markets offering facilities that range from the sophisticated sports centre to the various kinds of accommodation catering for those city dwellers who search for peace and relaxation in an atmosphere of great natural beauty;

(b) search constantly for ways of extending the season;

(c) be capable of development without spoiling one of the last great, un-spoiled, beautiful landscapes of Europe.

23. **Fishing** is very important where it really counts and that is largely in certain island and other communities where the tradition is still strong and where processing of the fish can be the basis of a land-rooted industry. The Board's plans for development of the industry take special account of this geographical significance.

24. **Manufacturing Industry** is the third main prop and we increasingly regard it as the most urgent of all relative to the immediate need to stem a substantial proportion of the emigration of talented sons and daughters from the Highlands and Islands. Forestry, in the public sector, is the job of a powerful organisation backed by Government policy and finance; and tourism is supported by the unquestionable appearance every year of more visitors. The problems in these sectors are really those of place and timing of development, level of investment and the communications to optimise them. But there has been no agency with the direct responsibilities and requisite powers to promote industrial growth in a thoroughly determined manner; and industrialists, unlike tourists, do not flood in voluntarily, or even through general publicity drives. It is our clear duty to see that this most important and most deficient element in the Highland economy is furnished; it should be recognised by all that we must devote a substantial proportion of our effort to it. Manufacturing industry is very poorly represented in the Highlands and Islands. Without it, the region will continue to lack any real possibility of a substantial enough rise in numbers to give credibility to Highland regeneration. Numbers are important in the justification or provision of all services internal to the Highlands and in major improvements in communications between the Highlands and the South. Modern industrial enterprises are absolutely essential in providing more of the kind of skills and initiative which will breed new enterprises and broaden the range of social and cultural leadership. Our policy in this field is, therefore, threefold:

we encourage the growth of industrial enterprise wherever a developer shows a personal and specific desire to settle or expand his enterprise;

we will pursue, however, a more methodical programme of building small industrial growth points in scale with the possibilities of the West and islands;

we will do our utmost to generate major growth points, involving substantial increases in population wherever the natural advantages of the area seem to warrant it; the Moray Firth is unquestionably the most important of these areas.

25. **Crofting** appears to be a form of living and working which gives deep satisfaction to those who follow it. It does not and cannot, except in rare cases, support the crofter as a full-time pursuit. It is fundamentally unstable, therefore, unless supplementary income is provided from other sources. Bearing in mind all that has been said about the system and its admittedly stultifying form of land tenure, it is apparently paradoxical (but, we believe, true) that if one had to look now for a way of life which would keep that number of people in such relatively intractable territory, it would be difficult to contrive a better system. Services maintenance and community viability are kept within the range of the possible, and even on the lowest estimate of its role, i.e., that of maintaining a living countryside in which the rest of the country can move, enjoy and recreate itself, it could claim justification. But its future continuance depends on other employment support. This the Board accepts as a clear challenge and duty; and one important element must be by way of small industrial growth points promoted by specially powerful and attractive inducements. Forestry and tourism must be the other aids in suitable places.

26. Two main comments are clearly necessary at the end of this broad statement of aims, and they have to do with certain fears expressed to the Board during the course of the year. One revolves around the whole question of the balance of policies between the Eastern and Central Highlands on the one Hand, and the Western Highlands and islands on the other. It may be

well at this point to quote from a paper prepared by the chairman for consideration at a Board meeting in March and which has been the foundation for subsequent Board discussions and meetings with various authorities, individuals and, in particular, with the Crofters Commission.

27. The paper says: "No matter what success is achieved in the Eastern or Central Highlands ... the Board will be judged by its ability to hold population in the true crofting areas". It goes on to analyse the possible methodology in pursuing the aim of a balance of priorities between East and West.

28. This difficult task is deeply rooted in the consciousness of the Board and colours all its actions. It is hoped that this will be accepted and believed by Parliament and the public, and that they will judge constructively and fairly on the actions and intentions of the Board as seen in this report. Elsewhere it is hoped that the reasonable fear of those who regard major industrial growth centres as a possible vortex sucking in population from the West and islands may be dispelled or, at least, mitigated.

29. The other fear is much bound up with those who are (again, reasonably) affected by headlines about "linear cities"—a meaningless phrase in itself but certainly not meaning ribbon development. Even if our most sanguine expectations and planning were to fructify in the industrial urban field, the amount of land taken up and the extent of influence on scenery and atmosphere would be minute. Moreover the vast bulk of the Highlands would remain visually as people know it except, simply, that there would be many more trees in its glens and moors, and more people either living in it or moving through it as visitors. And the Board is taking every step it humanly can to see that the bigger centres would be such that the country would be proud of them.

Editor's Note: Peter Peacock is a former leader of Highland Council, a Member of the Scottish Parliament and a Scottish government minister. In this commentary, he contrasts Professor Grieve's evaluation of the task ahead of the new HIDB, and reflects on how times and the agency have changed.

To read the first HIDB Annual Report is to read something very remarkable. Written by the first chair of HIDB, Robert Grieve, it reveals not only his stature and gravitas, it also reveals something more about a sense of confidence in the autonomy to act differently in the interests of a unique place, using an Act that 'gives great powers to this Board'.

The Foreword has the confidence to set the Highlands and Islands needs in a global context, and to comment on and challenge the attitudes and beliefs of Scots as they relate to the Highlands and Islands. These were not timid words, not set to defend a certainty of view but to set out the distinct needs of, and protecting the rights of, people in the Highlands and Islands to adopt a different approach.

The Challenges were honestly and clearly articulated: depopulation; the vulnerability of crofting; the balance needed between approaches to the East and the more challenging West; communications; and the danger of seeing the bare and spectacular landscape as some 'natural wilderness' when, 'in sober fact', it represented an ecological disaster. These remain core challenges today, despite all that has been achieved.

This first report reveals no development jargon, spin or adherence to central targets and national goals, nor any sense of a Board needing to look over its shoulder for approval. It is exactly the Board autonomy in policy and actions needed for the future: a unique region, unique challenges, still needing a unique and autonomous agency.

Peter Peacock, Inverness 2017

'Perhaps nobody was meant to notice…'

Brian Wilson

A long time ago, a young Brian Wilson benefited from the Highlands and Islands Development Board's support, when he and a group of university friends launched a radical local newspaper on the island of Skye, the West Highland Free Press. Years later, as a Labour Scottish Office minister, he appointed an SNP supporter, James Hunter, to the chair of Highlands and Islands Enterprise. That's just one of the things that wouldn't happen today, he says.

For the Nationalist-run Scottish government, eliminating the board of Highlands and Islands Enterprise must have seemed like just another administrative task, in line with the consistent objective of centralising all decision-making and funding distribution in Scotland as close to ministerial (and civil service) control as possible.

After more than 50 years of an autonomous economic development agency for the Highlands and Islands, there was to be no ceremony about its intended demise. Abolition of the HIE board did not merit a speech in Inverness, an announcement at Holyrood or even the issuing of a press release. Instead, it was slipped into an oral reply given by John Swinney, the Deputy First Minister, during a routine question and answer session. Perhaps nobody was meant to notice.

On 23 November 2016, Swinney referred to the outcome of an in-house 'enterprise and skills review'. Its conclusion was to bring Scotland's most prominent quangos – Scottish Enterprise, HIE, Skills Development Scotland, Scottish Development International, the Scottish Higher and Further Education

Funding Council – within the remit of one 'strategic body' under 'an overarching board'. Swinney added: 'Once established, the overarching board will replace individual agency boards while retaining the legal status of each of the bodies'.

Much of the Scottish media prefer to have their stories handed to them by government press officers. As a result, the most audacious act of centralisation in post-War Scotland went virtually unreported. (An honourable exception was the *Press and Journal* which has continued to wage an admirable campaign in support of the HIE board's retention). For those who did notice Swinney's startling intimation, the line about 'retaining the legal status' was not even seen as a sop worth having but as a device to avoid the need for legislation at Holyrood.

It is a reflection of how centralised post-devolution Scotland has become that there was no anticipation in Edinburgh that, once awareness spread, the HIE-related aspect of their masterplan would spark a widespread and furious response. Ministers knew they could rely on the abject silence of their own MSPs, who were elected to represent six of the eight Holyrood constituencies within the HIE area. And so it proved.

What they did not anticipate was the cross-section of other opinion within the Highlands and Islands who could see absolutely no good, and probably a great deal of harm, in the relegation of HIE to branch office status under an 'overarching' Scotland-wide board.

No organisation has the right to live for ever. The Highlands and Islands Development Board lasted just over a quarter of a century before being replaced with the more business-oriented HIE, which has now passed the same lifespan. So reform and re-focusing may be justified or, as I will argue, even desirable.

What Swinney's words signified, however, was not just organisational change but also a denial of the case on which a separate approach to Highlands and Islands issues has rested for half a century and, indeed, long before that through a panoply of legislation which recognised the cultural, social and economic distinctiveness of the Crofting Counties. Now all this was to be replaced by ideological pan-Scottishness, represented through an 'overarching' board.

Inconvenient Truths

For those of us who live on the Highlands and Islands periphery, and have sought to represent its interests over the years, it seems like the culmination of a long campaign to suppress inconvenient truths. The headline population statistics for the Highlands and Islands herald a great success story, and nobody need seek to gainsay it. Population within the region has risen. Living standards have been transformed. Great new industries have arisen. A wealth of opportunities has been created. Communications have been transformed.

All true – and the HIDB/HIE have played a major role in that process. If one reads only the headlines, then there is indeed a case for saying 'job done' and rewarding this achievement with subordination to an 'overarching board'. We are no longer the poor relations or the man on anyone's conscience.

But of course, headlines can distort the truth as well as report it. There are still large parts of the Highlands and Islands where the challenges which justified the establishment of the HIDB in the first place still prevail. They are still losing population. The vast majority of their young people leave. They are even more age-imbalanced now than they were half a century ago. Public services are struggling to support an ageing population. Employment is still elusive and, where it exists, often poorly-paid. The system of crofting tenure is little more than an empty shell. The new technologies and social amenities which might help retain active people struggle to keep pace with expectations. In short, there is still the same need for a public agency with strong interventionist powers, both social and economic, focused on the places which provide most of the popular images of the Highlands and Islands.

Those are the same places which, in his first annual report, Sir Robert Grieve identified as the ones by which the success or failure of the HIDB should be judged. That is still the crucial distinction. The good health of the Highlands and Islands does not correlate to the number of Tescos ringing Inverness or to the expansion rate of burgeoning housing estates in Moray and Nairn but to the state of peripheral communities in the north and west, the condition of which has all along represented the primary justification for the existence of a separate development agency. What consideration will they have in future, within the affairs of an Edinburgh-run, public sector behemoth under an 'overarching board', probably without a voice to represent them?

The point about the HIDB and (to a diminishing extent) HIE, has always been its ability to do things differently, to take more risks and to recognise the social context as well as the strict business case. All of this was enshrined in the founding legislation – the Highlands and Islands Development Act of 1965 – to which there had been a long preamble of discussion and reports about the need for such an agency. Without exceptional powers, there could be no economic transformation, so exceptional powers were granted.

True, they were not as extensive as first appeared. There was a widespread expectation that the new Board would be empowered to challenge the pattern of Highland land ownership in order to bring this primary resource into play for the benefit of the whole community. As it transpired, the land-related powers contained in the Act were much more unwieldy than advertised, and little came of them.

In other respects, however, the Board was given enormous scope in its ability to foster economic activity both in the most populated areas around the Moray and Cromarty Firths, and also in the islands through high-risk investments in fishing, tourism and other sectors which offered hope of growth. There were both successes and failures but it was widely accepted that a more cautious, conventional approach to economic development would have been of little use to places which had so little capital or confidence of their own.

My own experience of this willingness to accept both risk and controversy is instructive in demonstrating how much things have changed. Along with three friends from university, I founded the *West Highland Free Press* in 1972. It was quickly recognised as a journalistic phenomenon: a radical local newspaper which adopted the slogan of the Highland Land League – *An Tir, an Canan 'sna Daoine* / The Land, the Language and the People – and campaigned accordingly.

It was overtly political while also dealing with the bread-and-butter issues expected of a local newspaper: it dug into corners of local government that had remained hidden for decades; it exposed the follies of landlordism; and it brought serious journalistic scrutiny to bear on matters of public interest that would otherwise have gone unchallenged. It fervently supported the Gaelic language long before it was fashionable or profitable to do so.

For all of these reasons, it aroused hostility in circles of influence, as well as quiet support within communities that were unaccustomed to being spoken for in this way. The problem was that we had no money, and for two years the paper ran on the tightest of shoestrings. It could not have continued on that basis and no bank would have given us the time of day. By any conventional standard, it was a commercial basket case. Yet the HIDB, with a Tory government in office, had the vision, independence and courage to provide the investment support which allowed the paper to continue and a reasonably viable business to emerge.

For more than 40 years, because of that act of faith, it continued to provide employment and a public service. Is it conceivable that such a decision would be made today – or even less likely, in future, by Mr Swinney's 'overarching board' under political control in Edinburgh?

Arms-length Independence

Since the SNP came to power in 2008, the budget of HIE has been cut by 22 per cent and many of its powers removed. It is difficult to imagine it doing anything that might displease its political masters in Edinburgh.

Its Board is largely anonymous and its chairman has actually spoken in defence of what is now being proposed. All of this is unrecognizable for those of us who lived through the turbulent decades in which the HIDB and HIE were perfectly willing to exert their arms-length independence from government and to take stances which they believed to be in the Highlands and Islands' interest.

When they did so, they could be assured of cross-party support from politicians who had enough depth of experience and commitment to defend the interests of the constituencies and region, when required, rather than simply toe a party line. Would Donald Stewart, Russell Johnston, Hamish Gray, Charles Kennedy or Bob MacLennan have meekly acquiesced in what is currently being proposed, any more than I would, regardless of the political complexion of the government putting it forward? Most probably, they would have used their standing within their own parties to cut such nonsense off at the pass, before it ever saw the light of day.

The preferred line of defence – that HIE will continue to act as at it always has done, without a board – is both nonsensical and offensive to the memory of those who have gone before. Do those who argue in this way actually believe that the existence of a 'Board' has made no difference? Do they think that any of the courageous, unorthodox initiatives that HIDB/HIE have engaged in would have happened anyway, if there had not been people of stature to drive them through and, when necessary, stand up to the power of the civil service in Edinburgh in order to press their case in the Highlands and Islands interest? If so, they are either very ignorant or blind to history and the interests, past and present, of their constituents.

Time and again, the HIDB/HIE had to fight these battles in Edinburgh, often invoking the aid of both the Highland political lobby and public opinion in order to prevail. Without a board, HIE will have no such lobbying power, and the Edinburgh civil service – which has spent 50 years trying to curtail the independence of an autonomous and often troublesome development agency in the north – will finally have prevailed. Anyone with the Highlands and Islands interest at heart should be arguing for the restoration of greater autonomy – not the obliteration of the little that now remains.

I can offer one personal example of how things can happen through HIE that Edinburgh would only be interested in blocking. When Labour came to office in 1997 and I became Minister of State at the Scottish Office with responsibility for HIE, I was already due to attend the official handover of the island of Eigg to a community buyout. I phoned Iain Robertson, then chief executive of HIE, and said that I wanted them to establish a Community Land Unit to support buyout initiatives, and also an embryonic Land Fund so that there was a ring-fenced source of money to draw on. Iain had a project which needed my support and, though the words were never spoken, we did a wee trade-off. Fraser Morrison, the chairman, strongly supported what I was asking for.

Within a few weeks of the new government coming to office, I was able to go to Eigg and make these announcements with transformational implications for many communities. If I had tried to achieve the same outcome through Edinburgh, the initiative would have been bogged down – as others were – in months or years of delay and dilution. What interest, I wonder, would an 'overarching board' – its responsibilities stretching from university funding to foreign trade promotion, dominated by the voices of academia and the Central Belt – have had in such a peripheral Highlands and Islands cause? I am pretty sure I know the answer which is: 'None at all'.

Variations of that anecdote could be repeated many times over. Without leadership which is committed to certain outcomes, an organisation has no direction, and the people working for it will always be looking over their shoulder to where power actually resides. Thus the promise by John Swinney that Highlands and Islands Enterprise would retain its 'legal status' is worthless.

It is not 'legal status' that matters but the ability and willingness to make a difference. If the head is cut off, then the body will quickly wither – and, heaven knows, that process has already gone too far, to the point at which HIE needs not only saving but also urgent revitalisation.

The HIDB and HIE were, for many years, fortunate with their chairmen and prominent board members, some of whom had a long history of interest in the issue at hand – how to regenerate the Highlands and Islands. In that category, I think particularly of Prophet Smith, a Shetlander whose mission within the Board was to regenerate the west coast fishing industry. Ken Alexander, who became the third chairman in 1978, had been involved in drawing up Labour's plans for an HIDB almost 20 years earlier.

Not all of the chairmen were popular appointments. Sir Andrew Gilchrist, a retired ambassador, and Robert Cowan, a Hong Kong banker, were unknowns within the Highlands and Islands when their names emerged. But they became true converts to the cause of the Highlands and Islands. The implicit idea that none of these people was necessary to the work of HIDB/HIE and that the same organisation could have existed

– or could exist in the future – without a board to lead it is as disrespectful as it is misguided.

The Same Names

The chairman and leading board members of HIDB/HIE used to be big figures in the public life of the region and, indeed ,of Scotland. Today, hardly anyone could put a name or face to their successors. Acquiescence and anonymity are the credentials which are now most valued. Under the current administration, it would probably be like that, anyway. But the process was greatly facilitated by the Nolan reforms of the mid-1990s, prompted by a series of minor scandals surrounding public appointments under the government of John Major.

On the face of it, the Nolan reforms were beyond reproach. Political patronage was to be replaced with an open system of appointments made by independent panels. In fact, the outcome was to place enormous power in the hands of the civil service who would short-list 'appointable' individuals for ministers to approve before a final decision was taken.

I found out how this worked when I was in the Scottish Office. Time and again, the same names would be put forward, no matter which quango was involved. Time and again, ministers were told that individuals whom the civil servants did not like the look of had been deemed 'not appointable'. Battles were fought (not least over the appointment of Jim Hunter as chairman of HIE) but that required strong ministers and constant challenging.

Overall, the effect of Nolan, certainly in Scotland, has been to produce a magic circle of quangoteers, hand-picked by the civil servants. Some of the regular names which were being touted 20 years ago are still around, floating invisibly from one quango to the next. Far better when politicians could appoint individuals of calibre, then stand or fall by their own decisions – and that has certainly been borne out in the Highlands and Islands.

The relentless drive for centralisation should have been challenged more forcibly before now. In order to do so, however, it is necessary to see that each action is part of an overall strategy and that the whole is greater than the sum of the parts.

The most serious warning sign came when, in 2010, the Scottish government abruptly shut down the Highlands and Islands Partnership Programme which, since the mid-1990s, had been the advisory body on distribution of EU funding within the Highlands and Islands. It had representation from HIE, local authorities and other relevant agencies, as well as a deep knowledge of needs, priorities and how European funding could be leveraged to achieve them.

Since its abolition, all of these decisions have been taken in Edinburgh, and the funding earmarked in Brussels for the Highlands and Islands has been subsumed into a Scotland-wide pot. It is now re-badged as Scottish government largesse with the scantiest possible acknowledgement of its EU provenance, and there is a complete lack of transparency about where and how the money is spent.

Given how important EU funding had been to the Highlands and Islands over the previous 20 years, I found it astonishing that this was allowed to happen with so little political protest or recognition of its significance. Perhaps now it can be seen as the precursor of the superquango, the overarching board and the erosion of Highlands and Islands distinctiveness.

In the late 1980s, the Tory government produced changes to the HIDB which were more in line with it own ideological position. These started with the name – Highlands and Islands Enterprise sounded grittier, less statist and more business-like. They also established a network of Local Enterprise Companies to which much of the HIE budget was devolved. These turned out to be a very good thing, at least in localities which suffered from even Inverness being too far away to have much real understanding. (The LECs were abolished by the incoming Nationalist government in 2008.) Perhaps most critically in the longer term, the Tory reforms included an expansion of the HIE area.

Previously, it had consisted of the seven Crofting Counties and nowhere else. This built on the previous correlation between the crofting counties and the term 'Highlands and Islands'. The Clyde islands were brought in, which did not make a huge amount of difference. But so too were the counties east of Inverness – Moray and Nairn – which proved to be of very great significance. Apart from anything else, their populations far outweighed those of the mainland and islands periphery.

Strategically, a case could be made. Clearly, the Inverness conurbation was moving eastwards, and advocates of expansion believed it logical that HIE's writ should run within the whole of that area. However, the more Inverness grew, the more the balance of HIE's budget and board has shifted eastwards. American life science companies and a university campus do not come cheaply.

This trend has exacerbated rather than created a conflict which has existed since the earliest days of the HIDB. At that time, great emphasis was placed by Sir Robert Grieve – a distinguished planner – on the growth point strategy, which essentially meant creating major industrial hubs around the Moray and Cromarty Firths, and in Lochaber, as the centre-pieces of the new Highland economy. The problem with this was that the first places these centres were likely to draw labour and families from were precisely those peripheral Highlands and Islands communities whose declining fortunes had been seen as the primary justification for establishing the HIDB in the first place.

There is no clear-cut answer to this conundrum. Nobody would dispute the case for creating industrial activity in Easter

Ross, around Inverness and Lochaber. If people did not leave the crofting areas to go to these places, they would leave them to go to somewhere else.

The question is one of balance – and at what point public money should stop being used to further expand the Inverness/ Easter Ross conurbation when it might instead be spent on the more deep-seated needs of the Highlands and Islands periphery. After all, nobody could seriously argue today that the Invernessian is 'the man on Scotland's conscience' to quote Willie Ross's phrase which he applied to 'the Highlander', when setting up the HIDB.

Moving Out

On these grounds, I do believe that the focus of HIE should be moved quite decisively towards the periphery. That is not, in itself, enough. What the complex needs of these places demand is an integrated approach involving the full range of public bodies. Housing, land use and crofting regulation are the kind of synergies that matter, alongside the existing job creation remit of HIE – not university funding and foreign trade. It is a completely different paradigm to the one which Swinney is advancing through his overarching superquango. One size does not fit all in Scotland, or indeed within the Highlands and Islands.

An obvious candidate for this treatment would be the Crofting Commission, a singularly useless body which regulates decline from a remote outpost in Inverness. When the HIDB was being set up, some of its advocates argued for the Crofters Commission (as it then was) to be brought within it as a regulatory branch. This was recognition that crofting regulation, economic development and population retention in these places cannot be put into separate boxes. That lesson should finally be learned, the Crofting Commission wound up (to the shedding of very few tears) and incorporated into a new HIE structure.

When in Government, I tried to promote the same philosophy by establishing *Iomairt aig an Oir* (The Initiative at the Edge) which was intended to break down organisational silos and create unified public sector approaches at a very micro level to the needs of peripheral communities. This was fiercely resisted by the occupants of the silos and, without ongoing political commitment, nothing much ever came of it. Since then, there has been the spread of community land ownership, which could also be a far more effective factor in some of the most challenging areas if it was embraced as part of this integrated approach to detailed needs of specific communities.

So those of us who argue for the retention of the HIE board are not wallowing in nostalgia or doggedly defending the status quo. Of course there is a case for review and reform. But let it be creative reform, which respects history and diversity. Let it be imaginative and responsive to the needs of communities. Let it focus on those parts of the Highlands and Islands which still suffer from some of the same historic curses that applied in 1964. Let us devolve power and decision-making rather than relentlessly centralise them, under political control.

Or is all of that simply too much to hope for in a land where devolution stops at Edinburgh and radicalism appears to consist of creating overarching organisations to which the word 'Scotland' can be appended?

We shall see.

'It is only in winter that you notice so many homes with no lights on'

Michael Foxley

Whether as crofter, campaigner, councillor or even family doctor, his career in the Lochaber area has been inextricably linked with the work of HIDB and HIE. Here Dr Michael Foxley, a former leader of Highland Council, takes the pulse of the Highlands and Islands, assesses its economic and cultural health, the role HIE has played – and sometimes not played – and what the prognosis is for the future.

Knoydart, a West Highland peninsula just south of Skye and north of Mallaig, was once part of the kingdom of Somerled, the Gael of Norse descent who, in the mid-12th century, established himself as the first Lord of the Isles. It was subsequently ruled over by various septs of the Clan Donald.

The peninsula is beautiful but remote, and the terrain is harsh, giving rise to its Gaelic name, *na Garbh-Chrìochan* or 'the Rough Bounds'. To get there, you face the choice of a 16-mile scramble through some of Scotland's highest mountains, or a journey by boat across Heaven and Hell, the English translation of the two sea lochs Nevis and Hourn surrounding Knoydart. Today, it's popular with hill walkers and climbers.

But Knoydart has experienced a ruinous history. Following Culloden, the population suffered unspeakable cruelty when visited by the British Army and the Royal Navy. A century later, there was a final clearance of Knoydart. Already over 1,000 people had emigrated to Canada, but 500 remained. The people were dragged from their houses, which were then destroyed.

Some took to the hills and returned to build shelters, only to have them pulled down. Knoydart was then virtually empty.

In the 1930s, the estate was owned by Nazi sympathiser, Lord Brocket. During World War Two, it was requisitioned for the war effort but, disgracefully, Brockett got the land back after hostilities ended. In 1948, the Knoydart Land Raid took place, when a party of crofters marked out sites for new crofts, in an invasion immortalised in the song 'The Seven Men Of Knoydart' and commemorated today by a cairn. They received interim interdicts, no support from the Government, and finally they had to abandon their claims.

Thereafter, what remained of the original, massive Knoydart estate of over 100,000 acres was bought by property developers Rhodes and Lawson. They dismembered the estate and it was sold off in parcels. Immediately after the Falklands War in 1982, the Ministry of Defence took an interest in Knoydart. World War Two commandoes trained in and around the Spean Bridge area, and perhaps the idea behind the MoD interest in the peninsula – headlined in newspapers south of the border as 'the Last Great Wilderness' – came from similar roots.

There was public outcry at the idea of Knoydart becoming a military playground, so an environmental charity, the John Muir Trust – named after the Scot who invented the concept of America's National Park movement – was set up by former athlete Chris Brasher and Nigel Hawkins, among others. They intervened with the Secretary of State for Defence, Michael Heseltine, and the plan was dropped.

The new John Muir Trust, pledged to campaign for land rights and to support communities who wanted to take control of their own destiny, subsequently bought land on the peninsula, next door to what was to become the Knoydart Foundation.

That last 17,000 acres of Knoydart was now owned by jute company Titaghur whose chairman, Reg Brealey, planned to establish a 'Back to Basics' training school for the deprived youth of Britain's inner cities. This was bitterly opposed by most people in the 70-strong community.

In March 1994 I chaired the Highland Council planning committee visit to Inverie, the main settlement on the peninsula, after the Titaghur proposal was refused planning permission. The local residents made it plain that they wanted to run the place themselves. Mr Brealey, though, had other ideas, and he decided that Knoydart should be entrusted to businessmen Stephen Hinchliffe and Christopher Harrison. Their respective roles as chairman and finance director of the Facia retailing empire, which collapsed in 1996 with debts of more than £100 million, were then being investigated by the Serious Fraud Office and the Department of Trade and Industry.

Harrison ended up in prison in Germany for fraud involving German shoe companies. In October 1998, Knoydart Peninsula Ltd, the company that owned the estate, went into receivership with debts of £1.4 million. The following month, Mr Hinchliffe was banned by the DTI from holding a company directorship for seven years and was subsequently sent to prison for conspiracy to defraud. The company fell into the hands of the principal creditors, the Bank of Scotland, who wanted shot of it – fast.

What followed was a coming together of apparently strange bedfellows to wrest control of the Knoydart Estate into the hands of local people. We had to find the money to buy the estate. The resident population joined forces with local councillors like myself and my colleague Charlie King. Others piled in.

Chris Brasher was one of the pacemakers when Roger Bannister broke the four minute mile barrier in 1953, and was the man who founded the London Marathon. A fervent hill walker, he helped set up the John Muir Trust, who were also there. So was Chris, typically yomping into Inverie over the 3,000-foot high hills of the JMT's neighbouring estate while the rest of us northern softies came in by boat.

The sale price for Knoydart was £750,000. As main creditor, the asset was by now owned by the Bank of Scotland. The Knoydart Foundation – representing the community and the other interests – was launched at a meeting in the Bank of Scotland's offices at the Mound in Edinburgh. Present at this critical meeting were local councillor Charlie King; Nigel Hawkins, who led the John Muir Trust; lawyer Simon Fraser; and John Hutchison, who was Highland Council's Lochaber Area Manager. These people turn up a lot in this story.

They agreed a funding package: £25,000 from the John Muir Trust; £200,000 from the Chris Brasher Trust; £100,000 from another donor, the Betchton Trust, headed by a friend of Chris Brasher; and the Government's conservation agency Scottish Natural Heritage offered £50,000.

They were joined by the musical impressario Cameron Mackintosh, producer of such shows as 'Les Miserables', 'Cats' and 'The Phantom of the Opera'. Initially Sir Cameron, who has a west Highland retreat on Loch Morar, wanted to buy all of Knoydart and lease the land back to the community.

But, after a heated community meeting, that offer was rejected. The local people wanted no more lairds, no matter how well-intentioned. Cameron walked away, but then relented and promised to support the residents by matching whatever HIE was prepared to pay. That turned out to be £20,000, so the final package was £640,000 – still £110,000 short.

Highlands and Islands Enterprise had, in 1991, succeeded the Highlands and Islands Development Board at the behest of a Conservative government. Whether the new ethos would see the agency supporting what was, in essence, a public buyout, was something nobody knew for sure. But HIE came up trumps.

The man who was to become the elected chairman of the Knoydart Foundation took the initiative. As it became clear at the Mound meeting that the local bid was falling short, Charlie

King – the peninsula's local councillor – went to a side office in the bank.

His call was to Iain Robertson, the then brand new Chief Executive of the brand new HIE agency. At this point, HIE had created the Community Land Unit, and Knoydart was the first large case with which it had to deal. The new agency was reluctant to invest large amounts in community land purchase, preferring to consider assistance to development after the acquisition.

It had adopted a 'last brick in the wall' approach to funding community buyouts, and contributions tended to be in the lower thousands. But internal discussions were identifying that the community land movement was growing, with ministerial encouragement, and that this had the potential of a transformational impact, especially in remoter rural areas.

Already, people in HIE – even under new political management – were beginning to think that this 'last brick' formula might not be sufficient to ensure that community buyouts actually happened. They would have to be bigger bricks. The pressure to increase HIE's contributions grew, enhanced by effective lobbying from activists.

Charlie King's phone call therefore was tense, probably at both ends of the line. But in the end, Charlie cajoled and finally persuaded Mr Robertson to increase HIE's contribution from £20,000 to £75,000.

Charlie says that HIE's contribution was the 'most crucial', as it also brought in the equivalent matched funding from Sir Cameron MacKintosh – true to his word – and thus met the agreed sale price of £750,000. The money had been raised. The people took over.

Charlie King was quoted after the sale went through in March 1999: 'We have created history here today. Knoydart was possibly the worst example of land abuse in Scotland. We hope that what we have done will provide an example for others to follow and also show the path for the new Scottish Land Reform Bill.' It has.

HIE contributed a further £75,000 to draw up management plans to restore the run-down estate. The rest of the cost of the £750,000 management plan was shared by the local people, the Trusts, Scottish Natural Heritage and Sir Cameron MacKintosh. The lesson had been learned from the purchase of Eigg, two years earlier, that funding was as critical for the initial community developments as it was for the purchaser.

Back in Knoydart today, this is what has been achieved since then by the Knoydart Foundation: an increase in the population of almost 60 per cent, with more children in the school; more jobs; more businesses; more houses; and more investment and a major upgrade and repair of the vital estate hydro scheme. Knoydart is now run by its own people. That achievement is due, at least in part, to an agency that was prepared to go out on a financial limb to help make it happen.

As the former company secretary of Knoydart Foundation, John Hutchison, says: 'The support and advice from HIE, particularly at board level in the early days of the Foundation was very valuable, as was their assistance with the complexities of EU funding, to take forward projects such as the refurbishment of the hydro scheme.'

Mallaig: On The Road To The Isles

It may be at the very end of the A830 'Road To The Isles', but the settlement at Mallaig could very easily have become a forgotten community had it not been for the efforts of some formidable local campaigners, the Council – and Highlands and Islands Enterprise.

All Mallaig's development plans, studies and outline business cases in the last 25 years have been partially or fully funded by HIE. Without these plans, Mallaig would not have expanded, and may perhaps have contracted. These developments include the following: the steamer pier; the outer breakwater and harbour; the fisherman's net store; environmental improvements; and the linkspan, a type of jetty which enables roll-on roll-off ferries to dock safely.

The imminent opening of the bridge to Skye in 1995 meant that Mallaig had to mount a campaign to improve the ferry link to Armadale in the south of Skye. We had just over a year to work with HIE and Highland Regional Council, as it was then, to establish the linkspan, and a viable ferry service, in order to compete. Calmac made £2 million available to pay for the linkspan.

The fish feed building, with HIE and EU funding, allows feed company EWOS to ship tonnes of food for fish farms through the port, which is now the main distribution hub to salmon farming sites on the west coast of Scotland. HIE are now contributing 20 per cent of the cost of developing the new £90 million master-plan, together with Highland Council and the Nevis Estate, for the next ten-year phase of expansion.

Charlie King, who chairs Mallaig Harbour Authority, says: 'They were first class and wanted to see the community expand, as well as to promote economic development'. Robert Macmillan, chief executive of the Mallaig Harbour Authority, has no doubt. 'HIE have been vital for the sustainability of Mallaig harbour', he reckons.

Mallaig also now boasts a yachting marina, which was completed in September 2011. It's a £950,000 development, with berthing for 48 yachts with water and electricity available, financed by the Harbour Authority, Highland Council – and HIE. And it was a trans-national project, involving the Highlands, Northern Ireland and County Donegal, through a 256 million euro EU programme, called the Sail West initiative. These trans-national projects have been of vital importance to the Highlands over the past 25 years, and are seriously at risk after the Brexit vote of June 2016. Scott Dingwall, head of regional development for HIE, says: 'Sailing and marine tourism are growing industries and are making a huge contribution to the economies along the west coast'.

Sail West also contributed heavily to the Lochaline harbour and pontoon facilities. Lochaline, in Morvern, is a small village of only 300 residents, but the local people have a positive, entrepreunerial attitude to development, especially since they were omitted from the Scottish Office 'Initiative at the Edge'. They described themselves at the time as being 'over the edge'.

The village had strong support from HIE and the EU Leader programme. The marina provides 24 visitor berths within a short walking distance of Lochaline. A subsequent initiative established superb shore facilities, with showers, common toilets and laundry facilities. HIE were there every step of the way.

Salmon Farming: HIDB's Gamble

Salmon fishing isn't an area exactly free of controversy, and some people oppose the industry in savage terms, even today. But it has been a success story in the Highlands and Islands, and particularly on the west Highland coast, where many have been able to stay home because of the jobs that have come with the industry. Much of the credit for that, particularly in the early days, goes to the HIDB and its successor agency HIE.

What has made the west coast such a magnet for the industry is, of course, waters that are clear, pure and relatively free of pollution, as well as its sheltered sea lochs and coves. But what we also had back in the 1960s and the early 1970s was a government agency willing to take a gamble in backing its own judgement about fish farming.

Back then, the HIDB first sent two staff members to Denmark in 1966 to have a look at that country's fish farming industry. Two years later, there were various experiments running in Highland sea lochs. Plaice was being grown at Ardtoe, near Loch Moidart. Way up the west coast at Kinlochbervie in north-west Sutherland, skin divers were being used to farm lobsters underwater. But it was salmon where the greatest bonanza beckoned. This was the king of fish, closely identified with the Highlands and Islands, of course, but usually only available either to those prepared to fork out angling fees or, indeed, the occasional west Highland poacher. Certainly, in the shops salmon went for *de luxe* prices.

HIDB leaders were prepared to bet that salmon aquaculture would, however, work in the west, and that it would fit perfectly into the crofter lifestyle. It is capable of being combined with the various agriculture tasks on the typical holding, thus boosting crofters' income. They were to market this initiative with the suggestion of a fish farm 'at the foot of every croft'. That hasn't happened, but we now produce tens of thousands of tonnes of fish on Highland salmon farms. Thousands of people now work in the aquaculture industry, and many more depend on it for at least part of their income.

So, salmon farming started in Lochaber with an initiative in the early 1970s at Lochailort by Unilever. Loch Ailort is a sheltered sea loch adjacent to Inverailort Castle, then owned by Mrs Cameron-Head. The Castle was commandeered during the World War Two by the army, then used as a training base for the Special Operations Executive, and subsequently became a ship. At least, it was rechristened HMS Lochailort when the Royal Navy took it over to train would-be naval officers. The grounds still contain a number of buildings used by the Special Forces.

In 1973, the HIDB began to support salmon farmers with grants. In 1975, Marine Harvest opened a second fish farm in Loch Leven. In 1977, Inverness College – now part of the University of the Highlands and Islands – joined forces with HIDB to begin their first aquaculture courses. By 1985, HIDB had put more than £23 million into the industry.

Over the decades, salmon farming has become an integral part of the economy of the Highlands and Islands. Initially, salmon farms provided a significant number of jobs in remote areas. I carried out a survey in 1989 which showed that, within my then Regional Council ward of West Lochaber, outwith Mallaig, salmon farming directly employed one in four of the working population.

These days, the number of people working on the farms has diminished. For example, the salmon farm at Ardgour in the Ardnamurchan Peninsula, which used to employ ten local people, now employs eight.

The notion of a crofters' industry also fell prey to the world of high finance. The industry has changed hands several times, and is now owned by Norwegian companies. I do think this is a cause for concern. I believe that it does matter who owns the industry. Although this is now an international business, salmon farming in Norway developed in several communities as joint ventures with local companies, which might have been a better option here. Still, there's been plenty of local enterprise involved in the industry, even if big businesses have taken control, and Scotland is now the third largest producer of salmon in the world.

The future of salmon farming is moving offshore, to minimize pollution and try to combat the consequences of sea lice infestations. A recent initiative has seen the establishment of a large, well-managed salmon farm just offshore of the Isle of Muck, now in private ownership. The farm has created nine full-time jobs, and that will provide a healthy increase in the population. Fish farm operators Marine Harvest have built four houses for the workforce, and the houses will revert back to the community when they are no longer needed by the company.

Over the decades, the industry has suffered a number of disease problems, usually when the companies' accountants thought that doubling production would double their profits. There are limits to growth. Due to community concerns, the fallowing of sites – leaving them without cages, allowing the sea beds to recover – and the whole loch system management of a group of fish farms was invented in Loch Sunart.

But fish farming has provided many indigenous Highlanders with reliable employment over the past four decades, allowing them to stay in their local communities, build homes and raise families. In 2017, Marine Harvest Scotland forecast harvesting 55,000 tonnes of salmon, 85 per cent of this through their facility in Mallaig. They will also put about 9.5 million salmon smolts (young salmon) to sea through Mallaig port during the year.

Steve Bracken, the Business Support manager with fish farmers Marine Harvest, says: 'The salmon industry is still relatively young. Since that first harvest of 14 tonnes at Loch Ailort in 1971, we've learned greatly, having made mistakes on the way, which I think is only natural for a new industry.

'The important point is we've learned from these mistakes, and today the Scottish industry is producing over a hundred and sixty thousand tonnes of salmon. We've become the second largest food export from the UK.'

HITRANS: Come Back, HIE

The Convention of the Highlands and Islands – the extra-parliamentary grouping of Scottish government ministers, MSPs and local authorities – in 1996 set up the Highlands and Islands Transport Forum to discuss transport matters. Membership of the Forum comprised the chair of transport and the senior transport official from each Local Authority; the Head of Transport from Highlands and Islands Enterprise; the Director of the Scottish Council, Development and Industry (Highlands & Islands); and senior civil servants from the Scottish Office.

The Transport Scotland Act 2005 established regional transport partnerships across Scotland, with the duty to prepare regional transport strategies, including a delivery plan prioritising projects for investment. HITRANS (The Highlands and Islands Transport Partnership) was constituted in 2006 and replaced the Forum. Its members are the five constituent councils (one member from each) and three other members, to be appointed by the partnership. HIE was no longer a constituent member.

The Highlands and Islands is the only region in Scotland where road, rail, ferry, and air are all used for day-to-day transport of goods, services and people. So, they each present different problems, with consequently different solutions. The economy of the islands depends on ferry transport and air services which are expensive and vulnerable to poor weather. Road and rail links for the mainland economy are long and slow, involving journeys of over five hours to connect with the main Scottish centres.

The reliability and improvement of transport connections is one of the main concerns of the region's business community. The regional transport network continues to have deficiencies in journey times, and high costs in moving goods and people to Scotland's main economic centres. Examples are the A82 and A83 trunk roads, linking the west Highlands with the Central Belt, and the Inverness to Perth single-track railway line.

The island communities and many remote parts of the mainland rely on 'lifeline connections', which need to be strong and resilient. In some areas, these continue to be fragile and require urgent investment. Examples are the Western Isles single-track spine road and the Orkney internal ferry service.

HIE does not use its capital resources (around £30 million per annum) to invest in new transport infrastructure. However, it has supported specific initiatives, for example a £500,000 start-up grant to the current Inverness – Amsterdam air service.

In earlier days, HIE had a board member on HITRANS and helped to fund a lot of the lobbying initiatives: regional air service improvement; the Skye air service; the A82 and A9 north of Inverness; lobbying in both Parliaments on Public Service Obligations and Heathrow services; and others. HIE is now much less involved in transport matters than it once was, and generally there is a feeling that they could do much more, if they took an interest.

In view of the relationship between good transport connections and the competitiveness of the regional economy, the economic development agencies, along with the local authorities, were founder members of the original transport forum. It is regrettable that HIE has not been more forceful in seeking to have a member appointed to the HITRANS board. Officials continue to contribute to the group of advisers working with the HITRANS executive team, but again regrettably are no longer represented at director level within the organisation.

This is an area where HIE could, and should, do more: it ought to be a future priority. Just listen to those who've been at the sharp end: 'If the authority of the regional development agency is diminished, for example by amalgamation with a Scotland-wide organisation that has less empathy with the Highlands and Islands', says Howard Brindley, a former chief executive of HITRANS, 'then HIE will be a less effective partner in making the case for investment in the transport infrastructure of the region.'

'There is a direct relationship between improving the economy and improving the transport links in the Highlands and Islands', says Charlie King, a past chair of HITRANS.

HIE – and their paymasters – should be listening.

Fèisean: From Barra to Blas

The Gaelic word *Fèis* (festival) is synonymous with the community movement which, for over 30 years, has been tutoring traditional music, Gaelic song and Gaelic drama, and which boasts an impressive track record of opportunity and achievement for young people.

The movement grew from its beginnings in Barra in 1981, expanded into Ross-shire, Skye and Lochaber in the mid- to late-1980s, and experienced further rapid growth during the 1990s. The current year-round programme supports 47 *Fèisean* across Scotland, 23 of which are in HIE Fragile Areas, and it reaches over 71,000 people annually.

Having attended the three festivals in Lochaber, I have seen the vital role the *Fèisean* have played in building confidence and in using traditional music and Gaelic arts. We need to acknowledge that the national organiser, *Fèisean nan Gàidheal*, has contributed to a major change in Scottish cultural life, while the *Fèis* movement has probably had a much wider impact than can be measured.

Peter J Peacock, the former Minister for Education & Young People and Gaelic, says: 'The *Fèis* movement has clearly kept the language at the heart of its activity, and I believe that it is one of the best examples we have for promoting confidence in the Gaelic language. It is initiatives such as this that are needed to give Gaelic speakers the confidence to use and pass on their language and thus create a sustainable future for Gaelic in Scotland.'

Fèisean now employ annually around 400 individual musicians and singers to teach in communities and schools. *Fèisean nan Gàidheal* currently employs 12 people, and a report commissioned by HIE put the direct and indirect employment by the *Fèisean* at around 95 'Full Time Equivalent' posts. By 2015-16, the combined turnover of *Fèisean nan Gàidheal* and individual events had grown to £3.1 million.

Following a visit to Cape Breton's Celtic Colours by Highland Council's Chief Executive Arthur McCourt, the Chair of Education Andy Anderson, and I, we decided to start a Gaelic and Traditional music festival in the Highlands. After 12 years, the *Blas* Festival, delivered by *Fèisean nan Gàidheal*, has grown to become our premier annual festival, with local, national and international artistes appearing at many venues across the Highlands. HIE have provided financial support throughout.

Arthur Cormack, Mod Gold Medallist and chief executive of *Fèisean nan Gaidheal*, has this to say: 'HIE's support of the *Fèis* movement has been pivotal to the growth of our activities over the past 20 years. Its social remit makes it possible for HIE to put financial support into initiatives such as the *Fèisean*, and to support Gaelic more generally.

'Having HIE's support has allowed *Fèisean nan Gàidheal* to lever in funds from other bodies and, in doing so, deliver on HIE's social remit, as well as on economic targets. The potential benefit of Gaelic to the economy was recognised in HIE's research document, *Ar Stòras Gàidhlig*, and much remains to be done to fulfil that potential.'

Kinlochleven: No Graveyard Here

The village of Kinlochleven was formed from two separate settlements: Kinlochmore and Kinlochbeag. During World War One, it was the site of a POW camp. There is also the 'Navvies' Graveyard', linked to the village's most important feature.

In the early 20th century, Kinlochleven became a centre for the manufacture of aluminium, powered by the waters of Loch Leven held back by the long wall of the Blackwater Dam in three hills above the village. There you will find the Navvies' Graveyard, where some of those who worked on blasting chunks out of the mountains to construct the dam – many of the workers were Irish and some of them never properly identified – are buried under concrete markers.

The smelter, originally owned by the North British Aluminium Company and then by British Aluminium, employed at times over 800 workers, making a major contribution to the economy of South Lochaber for almost a century. With a strong international demand for aluminium, the village quickly grew to a thriving community of over 1,000 people. The smelter specialised in the production of high-purity aluminium.

However, in 2000 the owners, British Alcan, finally closed the smelter and a community trust was set up to save Kinlochleven. As the local arm of HIE in the area, Lochaber Enterprise created the Kinlochleven Land Development Trust, chaired by local councillor Drew MacFarlane-Slack and bringing together the community, Alcan, Highland Council and Scottish Natural Heritage. The Trust took control of the land and buildings left behind by the smelter.

The change today is stunning. The initiatives include: the former carbon centre became 'Ice Factor', a thoroughly modern climbing centre, which features a refrigerated wall for winter and ice climbing; a smaller building on the site became a brewery; four industrial units have been built on the site; the old chemical lab is now a bunk house; the new Trust took control of the run-down village hall, demolished it and built a new one; and there was a new campus for Kinlochleven High School, the primary school and the nursery, all sharing a new local library with the public.

Jackie Wright, then CEX of Lochaber Enterprise, recalls the impact of one of the initiatives. 'After the carbon factory was rebuilt, there was a large area of ground in front of it. We were also working with a group in Fort William on making compost out of fish and shellfish waste, mixing it with bark from BSW Timber's local sawmill. We had a huge pile of this compost at Corpach, and I suggested that it be used to make that bit of land at Kinlochleven suitable for planting up. The compost was taken down there and spread out. Within days, the whole village stank of rotting fish!'

HIE perhaps didn't initially understand the concept of community ownership and, when the Land Trust was thrown open to all residents of Kinlochleven, they did try to nominate members of the board. But they finally backed off and the Land Trust is now Kinlochleven Community Trust.

And that probably couldn't have happened in quite the same way had it not been for Lochaber Enterprise.

Eigg: The Electric Island

Twenty-five years ago, an air of decay hung over Eigg.

You felt it as soon as you stepped ashore onto the increasingly unsafe stone jetty. Blown over by the gales of many years, trees lay where they had fallen, strangling the life out of the island woods. It was an island frozen in the 1950s. There was little or no infrastructure, the landscape was littered with dilapidated houses which, despite their condition, still served as homes for the people, uncertain and apprehensive of their future.

In its earlier, turbulent history, Eigg had seen Christian priests massacred. It had been raided and settled by Vikings, and its entire population was massacred during a clan war. Then the new population of Eigg picked, through their clan chief, the wrong side in the 1745 Jacobite Rising, leading to some islanders being taken to London to die in prison and others being transported to Jamaica as slaves.

Clearances emptied large parts of Eigg, and when Keith Schellenberg took over in 1975 – narrowly outbidding the Highlands and Islands Development Board – there were few indigenous islanders remaining, the population supplemented by the laird, who brought in new people to work for the estate.

Schellenberg was an all-too-typical example of the sort of people who too often finished up as island lairds. A sportsman who won Olympic medals at bobsleigh, he was described as a 'buccaneering businessman' in the popular press of the day.

He was also the worst possible laird for an island community in the 20th century. He wanted no interference from the state or any of its organs which included, to the Council's own astonishment, the refuse department of Highland Council, which was barred from setting foot on Eigg to collect the bins. Living conditions for many of the islanders were close to intolerable, and the manner in which the island was run felt, frankly, almost feudal.

It took a long time to free Eigg of the Schellenberg name. First, his then wife sued for divorce, stating in a court action that the island was being devalued due to mismanagement. Then, islanders and some of their allies from elsewhere – including the broadcaster Lesley Riddoch and ecologist Alastair McIntosh – set up the Isle of Eigg Trust, with 73 per cent support from the community in a ballot.

In 1992, both the Trust and I, as Eigg's Regional Councillor, separately put together proposals to buy the island. I had prepared an outline business case and was seeking funding when Keith Schellenberg, using a property company, bought out his wife's share of the island. Schellenberg was back.

But not for long. The islanders and their laird were now pretty much at war. A vintage, yellow Rolls Royce belonging to Mr Schellenberg was destroyed in a mystery fire on the island. He tried to evict his farm manager, Colin Carr, and his family.

And when he sold Eigg, it wasn't to the islanders but to Maruma, a German fire artist, tactfully described on the Eigg web site as 'of doubtful credentials'. He had no evident means of support and no clear policy for the future. He appeared to want to use the island as a pawn in some unspecified international financial wheeze. He was, in the eyes of his new tenants, worse than his predecessor. He didn't last long.

The island was back on the market in 1996. The late Simon Fraser, a Stornoway solicitor who was to become the trusted navigator for the buyout and had previously worked with the crofters in Assynt, proposed a trust structure of a company limited by guarantee, with a membership of three organizations: the Island Residents' Association, with initial directors Maggie Fyffe, Karen Helliwell, Colin Carr (the farm manager) and Neil Wilcox; The Highland Council, with councillors Charlie King and myself; and the Scottish Wildlife Trust, with local representative Kenny Taylor. The Isle of Eigg Heritage Trust was formed, and immediately launched a public appeal to help buy the island.

There were distractions and counter-bids. The Pavarotti Foundation made an appearance, with the internationally renowned opera singer apparently intending to build an opera school on Eigg, with 3000 students from across the world. The Luxembourg company Compagnie de Participations wanted to set up a holiday development. And a failed Surrey banker wanted to farm the Island, despite still owing £10 million to depositors with his busted bank. The Heritage Lottery Fund refused to assist the buyout if the local people were to control the island. HIE also refused initially to help.

Simon Fraser had been involved five years earlier with the critical and successful Assynt buyout. In that instance, because of crofting law, 'nobody could put the Assynt crofters out of their homes', he said.

'Eigg was on a different plane emotionally, it was so incredibly important to all these people', he said later. 'It had the potential to turn all their lives around. The people were clinging on with no security of tenure, having to put up with leaking roofs and busted old generators. On Eigg, they *could* be evicted. The residents' lives were dictated by the whim of their landlord. There was no real money economy left on the island.'

A key turning point in the campaign was when the Carrs at Kildonnan were threatened with eviction. With a family of five, and no security over their home, farmhouse and farm, they were extremely vulnerable. This threat ensured that virtually the entire island supported the community buyout.

And, in the end, we won. The press and media flocked to the story and there was coverage across the world, with the plight of the islanders engaging the attention, and the financial support, of many people.

The island changed hands for £1.5 million, a sum of money made up of thousands of individual donations, including one major donation of £900,000 from a mystery benefactor in England, who contacted Trust secretary Maggie Fyffe out of the blue with her offer, on condition she was never publicly identified. It was a triumph, and it opened up the land reform process.

Simon Fraser – who was always a step ahead of the other side's lawyers – had no doubt about its significance. 'There is absolutely no doubt in my mind that the buyout of Eigg struck a major blow for the cause of land reform', he said. 'It was a thing that turned the corner and got the stone rolling. If the people of Eigg could do it, other communities could as well.' Subsequently, many have.

Highlands and Islands Enterprise were *not* major players, perhaps reflecting the views of their Tory paymasters at that time. But they did contribute the last necessary sum of £17,500 – the 'last brick in the wall', as the agency itself described it.

I have to admit that, as a director, I didn't want the money, thinking it would taint perceptions of what we'd done and that we'd be perceived as having been overly reliant on public funds. But Simon Fraser, ever sensible, persuaded me: 'We've bought the island', he said, "but we have no money to develop it.' We took the money.

HIE's importance to the development of Eigg came *after* the buyout. We soon realised that purchasing the island had been only the start of the project, and it was going to need substantial funding for further development. HIE, with other sources, assisted with funding towards appointing a project officer to oversee the changes required, to hire consultants, to do some marketing of the place, and to set up a website.

Islanders developed their own hydro schemes and subsequently electrified the entire island, introduced machinery to restructure the woodlands and, especially, constructed An Laimhrig, the vital multi-purpose centre which became home to the tea room, craft shop, toilets and office. Eigg had joined the 20th century.

Maggie Fyffe, the hardworking and determined secretary of the Trust says: 'Following the buy-out in 1997, HIE's assistance was crucial in helping to revitalise the island. Being able to employ a development officer was an essential part of this process, as was funding towards our first major project, building An Laimhrig, which improved facilities on the island immeasurably.'

The buyout was officially celebrated on the island on 12 June 1997 at an event led by the new Scottish Office minister Brian Wilson. It was a tremendous party and, during it, Mr Wilson announced the formation of the Community Land Unit, which was to support more community buyouts, and which would be based on Highlands and Islands Enterprise. 'Over the past thirty years, stewardship of this island has come to symbolize much that was wrong about the free market and land', he told the islanders, predicting that now the Community Land Unit would be a leader in a time of change.

I have to admit that, at the time, I argued with Brian that the land unit should not be based solely at HIE, as they hadn't been involved in the buyout. I thought it should have at least been jointly managed with the local authorities. But Brian prevailed, and the chief executive of HIE, Iain Robertson, returned from the celebrations a much happier man than when he'd first arrived, rather forlornly, on Eigg, a latecomer to someone else's party.

Subsequently HIE, through the Community Land Unit, were extremely supportive of land reform. The Unit was expertly managed by John Watt. They have helped many of the community buyouts in the Western Isles, for instance where 75 per cent of the land is now owned by the people.

Here is my own quote on that day: 'The long campaign to buy the Isle of Eigg was a roller coaster, but a superb example of Highland teamwork, involving virtually all of the residents; Highland Council officers and councillors; the Scottish Wildlife Trust; the media; the Scottish people; and our legal expert.'

Today, the island has been transformed. There is a splendid new jetty served by a modern car ferry, new housing, an increased population, and an air of determined confidence. The islanders' work on renewable energy has won national and international awards.

One family, to whom I refer earlier, symbolises the transformation of the Island. Colin and Marie Carr had no security of tenure for the farm, their guest house and the home for their five children, and had been served with an eviction notice. Marie's mother, Peigi, had no security of tenure at nearby Laig farm. They were in a very vulnerable situation. Today, Kildonan House Hotel has been beautifully refurbished, tenancies are secure and four generations of their family now thrive on Eigg.

UHI: The University is Everywhere

The Highlands and Islands have been campaigning, on and off, since 1653 for a university in the region. In the 1960s, Stirling was preferred to the Highlands as the location for a new Scottish university. But the issue didn't go away.

In 1991, the Highlands and Islands Development Board commissioned Professor Sir Graham Hills to report on how a Highland university might be achieved. Hills was a physical chemist who, as Principal of Strathclyde University, had helped save that institution at a time of cuts and had then expanded it.

His report confirmed the potential for a federal, collegiate university based on seven existing further education colleges. At the same time, an advisory group was formed from various stakeholders including HIE and the Highland Regional Council, as well as business bodies and Sabhal Mor Ostaig, the Gaelic college on the island of Skye. I was part of the Council delegation, led by Val MacIver, our determined and visionary chair of Education.

In 1992 the University of the Highlands and Islands Project was born. It was largely funded by HIE and the Council, leading to the creation of UHI Millennium Institute (the Millennium Fund gave us a grant of £2.5 million towards our headquarters), which became a higher education institution in 2001, and was granted its own 'taught degree' awarding powers in August 2008 after further funding of £5 million from HIE.

The University of the Highlands and Islands is now a partnership of 13 colleges with over 70 learning centres across the region. Ours is a very different university, whose reputation is built on our innovative approach to learning, and our distinctive research and curriculum – all enriched by the people, natural environment, economy, culture and heritage of the Highlands and Islands and its communities.

Our centres include:

SAMS: A major marine science research and training facility in Oban.

Inverness College: Now based in a new building on a campus east of Inverness City and built by HIE. It took some while to persuade them to relocate, especially during a memorable leadership meeting in Edinburgh with the College leadership who were then still determined to stay on the Longman Industrial Estate. They eventually saw sense, and Diane

Rawlinson, the new Principal of Inverness College UHI, says: 'Overall, HIE investment has produced a very high quality environment in which our College now sits.'

Sabhal Mor Ostaig: The Gaelic Medium College on the Isle of Skye is a superb achievement. Starting with a derelict steading on language activist Sir Iain Noble's island estate, and with initial strong support from the Council, the Highlands and Islands Development Board and the Western Isles Council, it initially offered short courses in Gaelic and traditional music.

It has steadily developed into a major campus, with over 70 full-time students, plus over 300 students taught through video and telephone conferencing and assisted by over £9 million of HIE funding in the past ten years. It has also more than doubled the population of the Sleat peninsula in the south of Skye, and transformed its economy.

As former Principal Professor Norman Gillies says: 'HIE support provides confidence, and then you secure another application for funding that's bigger and better, and that's the story of Sabhal Mor Ostaig.'

We also have colleges in the major centres of Perth, Elgin and Thurso, as well as colleges serving the rural communities of Argyll, Shetland, Orkney and the Western Isles.

But Colleges within the UHI are about much more, as I learnt from my 18 years as chair of Lochaber College, and then West Highland College (after we merged with Skye and Wester Ross College). It is also about retaining the oft-quoted 'missing generation' of 16-30-year-olds from the Highlands and Islands. Our young people used to leave for training at universities and colleges far away, and never came back. As Professor Jim Hunter so eloquently put it: 'Three or four good Highers and a grant were the equivalent of the emigrant ship'. Today, 75 per cent of students learning at the UHI are from the Highlands and Islands.

West Highland College developed over two decades from a collection of Portacabins in Fort William to ten learning centres across Lochaber, Skye and Wester Ross. We now ensure our people can access Further and Higher Education if, for caring or financial reasons, they need to remain near home. We give a second chance to our people who may have failed at school or drifted in early adulthood.

Access to a vocational course can build confidence, so that the student goes onto a Further Education course and then onto a job or a degree. As chair of West Highland College on Graduation, I have been thanked by parents, with tears in their eyes, for giving their son or daughter a second chance, and for awarding them a FE or HE certificate.

Well done, HIDB. And Graeme Hills.

Where We Are Now

My intention in this book is to look dispassionately at HIE, its predecessor body HIDB, and their record in aiding Highlands and Islands development. My casebook reveals some of their successes, but I would now like to address their failings and suggest scope for possible improvements.

The principal areas on which I here concentrate are land reform, energy, agriculture, the Gaelic language, rural deprivation and depopulation.

Land Reform

Willie Ross's speech to Parliament in 1965, when he announced the establishment of the Highlands and Islands Development Board, included this passage: 'We have, in the Scottish Highlands, nine million acres ... and we are short of land!

Clearly the board must have the power to acquire the land by compulsion if necessary, if it is to be effective.'

The HIDB got that power, but didn't use it. Peter Peacock, a past Highland Council Leader and Scottish government ex-minister, says: 'They never at any point seemed to challenge one of the most obvious and internationally peculiar aspects of the Highlands, namely the concentrated land ownership patterns. They had compulsory purchase powers on land but they have never been used.

'Why were they not used, for example, on Raasay or Eigg? Was it too politically controversial for them, or too difficult a task to engage the wrath of the land-owners?'

I remember Peter Peacock's determined support for the Assynt Crofters and their eventually successful buyout of their land in 1994. So does he.

'In the case of the Assynt buyout, when the council was approached for its backing, as the finance chair, I was very keen to give that support. Principally, because if the democratically elected body for the Highlands did not support people in a land struggle, given Highland history, we could not expect anyone else to do so', he says.

'At the time, HIDB were not volunteering to come forward (rather they saw their approach as <u>possibly</u> providing the "last brick in the wall', as it was put), whereas the council saw themselves as helping provide a lead – one of the "first bricks in the wall".

'What happened then was when the council declared support and put up the money, HIE, because of competitive behaviours (with the council), only then made funds available.'

This is the critical issue. It is not the 'last brick in the wall' that is needed with projects and buildings: it is the 'first brick in the wall'. I think this attitude has been a significant failure of HIE.

This 'first brick' will be essential if the Scottish Government's target of a million acres in community ownership in 2020 is to be achieved. They still have almost half a million acres to go. And less than three years in which to do it.

Having said that, once the land has been purchased the Community Assets team at HIE plays a critical role: to work with the community. This role needs to increase in the future, with the community empowerment bill and increased community ownership.

Energy

HIE, quite rightly, promoted the development of renewables, particularly offshore. They put a considerable amount of work and effort into funding research. So much so that Calum Davidson, the director of energy at HIE, had a massive offshore wind turbine named after him, to acknowledge the contribution he made to the marine power industry in Scotland.

However, much more could, and should, have been done to ensure that the procurement process for developing these major wind farms, by developers such as Scottish and Southern Energy (SSE), included the use of local firms, provided apprenticeships, and funded training through the UHI and multi-million pound community benefit. Also, the development of renewables still needs to be skewed towards community ownership. This would benefit local communities directly and would also provide cheap electricity for small- and medium-sized businesses (SMEs), especially in the Islands.

Agriculture

I have never really understood why HIE have not become more actively involved in agriculture. I led the promotion of Lochaber lamb and beef in 1999, a project based on the already successful

Orkney Island Gold marketing campaign. For two years we employed somebody to buy fat lambs at the local auction mart, have them butchered in the Highlands, and then sold direct to local hotels and restaurants, who would then indicate their local provenance on their menus.

But this project was obstructed by dealers, the mart and slaughterhouses, because it disrupted their existing arrangements. HIE and Europe funded it for two years but, after 2001, HIE ceased funding it.

Crofting agriculture is very heavily dependent on EU funding, and this support is, of course, now at risk because of Brexit. HIE has been silent on the subject, as they have on their expenditure on crofting development grants, access to crofter housing grants, and the serious risk to continuing subsidies for crofters.

Crofting keeps people in a living landscape in remote areas. It maintains land in good condition with biodiversity. And it provides high-quality store lambs and calves, while ensuring access where there is active hill management. It needs to be positively supported by the development agency.

Gaelic

I give credit to HIDB for their support to Gaidhlig through Sabhal Mor Ostaig, the Gaelic college on Skye, where all subjects are taught through the medium of the language, and for the support they offer the *Fèisean* movement. As the former college Principal Norman Gilles put it: 'The likes of (former HIDB officials) Bob Storey, Roy Pederson and Iain MacAskill lit a spark for the language'. And they made things happen.

Sabhal Mor Ostaig, as the national Gaidhlig college for Scotland, stands as a major success. However, HIE refused to become involved in the creation of Gaidhlig schools and Gaelic medium units in other monoglot schools, seeing it as the responsibility of the education authorities. However, these

Gaidhlig schools were also a community hub, many of them coming into being because the communities wanted them.

We managed to persuade HIE to make a contribution to the community facilities in the new Ardnamurchan High School, but it was disappointing that they felt incapable of doing that in the Gaidhlig schools which were, after all, significant community initiatives by those parents involved.

Another area in which HIE has failed the language is in their refusal to tie its use to grants. I have joined European officials and some of HIE's own officers in urging HIE to make it a condition of grant aid that businesses – especially tourist businesses – use bilingual marketing on their notepaper, vans, offices, etc, as was done in Ireland 30 years ago. The request was refused.

If that initiative had been supported, it would have created a major expansion to the rollout of bilingual signage throughout the Highlands and Islands, and demonstrate the importance of Gaidhlig as a living language. It is hard to see why HIE so strongly resisted this proposal.

Meanwhile, Brexit – the proposed exit of the UK from the European Union – is a major threat to our communities. I cannot think of a single significant project in the west Highlands that was not partially funded by European grants, like Leader or ERDF. When you started a campaign for a project, you knew automatically that you were going to receive somewhere between 10 and 50 per cent of the funding from Europe.

Additionally, if you remove the current EU citizen workforce, particularly Poles and Latvians, from the Highlands, there will be a major gap in the workforce in the salmon factories, NHS and hospitality industry. The Highlands and Islands have benefited from hundreds of millions of European funds, and has resulted in a leverage of probably four times that amount. It is very unlikely that any UK or Scottish government will reproduce that scale of regional aid in the future.

Highland Council and HIE used to share an office in Brussels for lobbying purposes, and the Highlands and Islands were always viewed very sympathetically by EU officials. So what now?

To quote Professor Robert Grieve, the first chair of the HIDB: 'No matter what success is achieved in the eastern or central Highlands, the HIDB will be judged by its ability to hold population in the true crofting areas'. This is as true today as it was then. It requires major effort and support to address the challenges in the remote and rural areas.

But HIE has become too bureaucratic. For example, I am a member on the Leader group for Lochaber, dealing with grant applications to that European programme which is administered locally by HIE. They have now made the process so complicated that we have decided that it's not worth applying for any grant less than £10,000. Many projects funded 20 years ago had a total value of less than £10,000, with Leader still making a significant contribution.

On community-owned land, HIE have insisted the local community representatives must be in the majority, which is praiseworthy if the full range of skills already exist there. What it meant in practice was that this policy forced the Knoydart Foundation to change their governance body and to shed one local councillor. The same stricture was attempted on Eigg, but strongly – and successfully – resisted, on the grounds that the structure had been established before HIE was involved.

Depopulation

HIDB was brought into being to fight depopulation and has been successful in some places, like the Isle of Skye which has seen a significant increase in population and business activity. Tourism is now such a major force in Skye that they are having to consider taking major steps to control and manage it. However, other areas have not fared so well.

Depopulation is still taking place in the Western Isles, Argyll, Caithness and Sutherland and in significant areas of the west coast. This depopulation is often hidden by the increasing presence of holiday and retirement homes in these beautiful localities.

It is only in winter that you notice so many homes with no lights on. In West Ardnamurchan over half of the housing stock is holiday homes. In some townships, holiday and retirement homes make up over 90 per cent of the stock. Someone selling a small house in London for £3 million can afford to buy two house sites on the west coast or – and this happens – a house and its neighbouring property in order not to have close neighbours.

We must consider rural deprivation. The cost of living in a remote rural area is at least 40 per cent more than in an urban area. Wages are lower and a car is essential. However, the measures to tackle inequalities are always targeted at deprived areas of cities which are listed in the Scottish Index of Multiple Deprivation (SIMD). These were often, in the past, dumping grounds for council house tenants who were seen as 'less than perfect', and that cycle has continued for decades. There is no acknowledgement being made as to the scale and extent of rural deprivation. It is essential that this is acknowledged and tackled in order to reduce inequalities.

The argument has been made for the islands, with their 'Our Islands, Our Future' campaign, which laid out the special case for Orkney, Shetland and the Western Isles, and the need to take account of their special circumstances in all Scottish government legislation. That case seems to be accepted by the Scottish government, but the campaign was put together by the local authorities, not HIE.

HIE now concentrates primarily on major business growth, which is frequently referred to as 'transformational'. One such development came early in 2017, when the company Liberty rescued the old British Aluminium plant in Fort William by buying it from Rio Tinto, thus safeguarding many well-paid jobs. However, that expansion now envisages around 1000 new jobs being created.

I am old enough to remember the pulp and paper mill arriving at Corpach near Fort William with, similarly, 1000 new jobs. Ninety-nine per cent of those jobs were filled by people from Aberdeen and Glasgow.

There is the potential for the same to happen again in Fort William, with a huge number of poor-quality houses being built rapidly to accommodate the inflow of essential workers, thereby creating another significant housing debt. As with so many other issues, some joined-up thinking is required.

Where We're Going

As a lifelong, home-rule Liberal, I voted for independence in the 2014 referendum, on the basis that decisions concerning Scotland were best made by people in Scotland. This principle should apply equally to decisions about the Highlands and Islands, which are best made by the people who live there, and who know and care about our region. We need to maximise the use of local expertise and knowledge and be responsive to the needs of the people of the Highlands and Islands. We need to be proactive.

Douglas MacDiarmid was CEO with HIE's local enterprise company in Lochaber. He says: 'We need to be like one of Nelson's frigate captains, who could set their own course and do whatever was needed to be done to make things happen'.

HIE have, in recent times, failed our region, with their emphasis on big business and their avoidance of assisting in key issues, such as crofting, Europe, Gaelic Education and smaller community initiatives. Now the Scottish Government wants to remove the HIE Board and introduce a 'Super Board' for Scotland, from the ashes of the Scottish Funding Council, Skills Development Scotland, Scottish Enterprise and HIE. I am dismayed that not one of our seven Highlands and Islands SNP MSPs have publicly spoken in support of retaining the HIE Board. At the time of writing, we may now have to accept the reality that this proposed new board will be a board for urban, Central Belt Scotland.

If that comes to pass, what should we campaign for? My view is that we need a new social enterprise body for the remote rural Highlands and the Islands. We need to restore confidence to these areas, with a devolved structure of offices and staff, with lessons learnt from Norway where they've been doing this sort of thing for years.

This new body needs to work in partnership with the local authorities, for the social and economic benefit of our rural communities, and based on partnership and teamwork. We need to maximise decision-making and funding to local communities.

So we should start by devolving to this new body the management of the Crown Estate in Scotland, which manages about half the country's coastal foreshore and all of the sea bed, as well as running four estates. The Crown Estate is due to be transferred to the Scottish government progressively from April 2017. With its headquarters based in a remote rural area, it should further devolve the management and funding from the Crown Estate to local harbours and local areas.

A century ago, the Highlands and Islands Medical Service came into being because of the dire state of medical services in the Highlands and Islands. They were 30 years ahead of the creation of the NHS which was largely modelled on the success of the Highlands and Islands medical service. There's a lesson here.

We need also to establish a body adequately to manage, assist and fund the remote and rural areas and the Islands. Other public agencies could join this new body, potentially a Rural and Islands Development Scotland (RAIDS), namely:

- The Crofting Commission, which is currently in chaos and at odds with its own chair. Crofting and Agricultural support in the crofting counties would then come from RPID, the Rural Payments and Inspection Division of the Scottish Government, who should understand that crofting is not an agribusiness.
- Scottish Natural Heritage and Deer Management, because of their impact on the lives and environment of our Region.
- HITRANS. Transport and communication are absolutely fundamental to the area. The expansion of Broadband, which has already been pioneered by HIE and British Telecom, should be intensified so that it reaches the most remote communities.
- All aspects of Land Reform.
- Creative Scotland's input to the Highlands and Islands.
- The government-owned ferry company Caledonian MacBrayne and its offshoot CMAL, which owns the ferries ports and harbours, and which has a poor track record of connecting Island communities.
- Highlands and Islands Airports Authority.
- Responsibility for Highlands and Islands SME business support. This is essential.
- UHI funding from what is presently the Scottish Funding Council, as our region is so very different from the other 12 in Scotland.
- Inshore Fisheries management.
- And finally Bord na Gaidhlig, the administrator of the language.

These public bodies all serve the islands and rural areas of the Highlands and Islands. We need to have a discussion with the Borders, and other rural areas of Scotland, about whether they want to join us.

By setting up this new body, the Scottish government would be making a strong commitment to the decentralisation of power to local communities. Governance would then be by people living and working in our region and within a federal structure.

We need a change for those who live and work in our region – and we need it now!

'The communities are here ... build on them'

Maggie Cunningham

Macro-management of the Highlands and Islands won't work. Seeking to integrate pan-national organisations with an area that is very different from urban Scotland, and then running them all from the centre, will not address the problems of the Highlands and Islands. Instead, argues Maggie Cunningham, we should be aiming to allow communities in the Highlands and Islands to identify what they need, and tailor service provision accordingly. Micro-management isn't a dirty word. One size doesn't fit all.

In a book called *Let not the Waves of the Sea*, by Simon Stephenson, a young man from Edinburgh goes to Thailand to retrace the steps of his brother Dominic who was killed in the devastating 2004 tsunami. He met a barman on the beach where Dominic died. The barman had lost his wife, children, brothers and sisters. He had perfected the following story for tourists who came to commiserate with him.

A water buffalo was friendly with two birds that lived on his back. One morning he was woken by the birds having a fight. He asked them to be quiet so that he could get back to sleep, and reluctantly they settled down, one on his back and one on his head. The storyteller asks his audience where they think the buffalo feels the most weight. After many unsuccessful attempts at the answer they turn to him and ask: 'Okay, where does the buffalo feel the greatest weight?' He replies: 'Who am I to know what a water buffalo feels?' It was his response to those who assumed that they understood his pain and his loss.

This story came to mind when I was listening one morning to the Highland news on Radio Scotland. A spokeswoman from NHS Highland was commenting on the challenge of recruiting GPs to locate to remote communities. She suggested that a big part of the problem was that GPs made a lifestyle choice to work in these areas. Therefore, it was important that, when they met in the local shop and other social settings, patients and others did not bother GPs with their ailments. Her homily was so crass that it had me sitting bolt upright in bed.

Contrast this experience with one I had a few weeks later at the funeral of a local stalwart. At her request, there was no formal eulogy, but the large numbers that turned out to pay their last respects spoke louder than could any words about her hard work, her kindness, her support for others and her irrepressible cheerfulness. When it was clear that there was no more treatment to help fight her cancer, she was touched by the fact that the local doctor at Broadford who relayed this to her had tears in his eyes.

What assumptions was the NHS Highland spokeswoman making, not only about how people behave in remote communities but also about doctors? What impact do those assumptions have on encouraging people to work and live in our more remote communities? Did she not think that it may have helped to have a stronger understanding of these communities before she opined so irresponsibly?

The Scottish Government recognises the importance of thriving communities in its Communities Empowerment Act of 2015. It is an important indicator of intent, which sits rather uncomfortably alongside the centralisation of police, fire and ambulance services. On one hand, there are valid cost-saving exercises in creating central bases for administration. On the other hand, when frontline services turn up in the wrong towns or villages because of communication blunders, or if the service is inferior to what has gone before, how can we believe the intent to empower communities has any substantial investment?

There is a precedent for 'Empowering Communities', especially in the remoter communities of the Highlands and Islands. *Iomairt air an Oir* (Initiative on the Edge) was the brainchild of Brian Wilson in 1998 during his time as a Scottish Office Minister. The idea of bringing all the public agencies together to create a one-stop-shop locally was a brilliant one, and it worked to a degree. The challenge for public agencies to genuinely buy in to partnership is often too great, as appeared to be the case here. Often, commitment to their own processes and bureaucracy becomes a greater priority than helping the communities they are set up to serve. Unfortunately, after Brian Wilson moved away, so did the political commitment, and without the perseverance of their political masters it seemed there was little incentive for public servants to enthusiastically commit.

There is a theory called the Five Cs of Partnership, which starts at a basic level of Co-existence and continues through a hierarchy to Co-ownership, where all parties commit themselves wholly to achieving a common vision and to making significant changes in what they do and how they do it. To genuinely serve our remote communities co-ownership and a move away from individual agencies is crucial.

In many ways, our public services have responded well to the needs of our smaller communities, and there have been phenomenal improvements on many fronts over the past 30 years. Community land ownership is a great success story in many places. The resurgence of Harris Tweed, better management of tourism, and the exploitation of North Coast 500 are a few other examples of this progress.

However, there is a danger that some of these developments are still just treating the symptoms, while the core problems of population decline and an ageing demographic continue, particularly in the more fragile rural areas.

While the Scottish Government has been 'sent homeward to think again' over its proposal to centralise the Boards of all the enterprise and skills agencies, including HIE, I wonder what might happen if it was willing to go back to first principles and to work out what exactly needs to be done to ensure that our remote and island communities are genuinely able to thrive.

The Horse Has Bolted

I believe that, by the time we are addressing community regeneration and identifying 'assets', the horse has bolted. We must take a 'cradle to the grave' approach to ensure genuine regeneration, because anything else is just treating the symptoms.

We must start with housing, and especially affordable houses for young families. However, one of the key initiatives unique to the Highlands and Islands appears to be failing. The purpose of the Croft House Scheme is to improve and maintain the standards of crofter housing, with the aim of attracting and retaining people in the more remote areas. Crofters are required to live on or as close to their crofts as possible, but crofting tenure makes it difficult to attract the standard type of mortgage for building or regenerating houses.

Figures released early this year show that the lowest number of successful applications was in the Western Isles, where the problem of housing is among the most acute. The same figures show only half the eligible applicants for grants were successful, which does not build confidence in the Government commitment to 'Empowering Communities'.

Over the years, criteria for qualification has become more and more rigorous and the number of hoops to be jumped through discourages and exhausts potential applicants, but unless young families can build houses on their crofts, how can we step back from the demographic cliff-edge that these islands are approaching?

Surely a holistic approach, starting with young families having decent housing, is the way to go? We must take a micro approach to micro situations, rather than a 'one size fits all' approach to governance of public bodies. If we have proper housing for young families, the next issue to consider is child care. For mothers who want to go out to work or start their own business, which is often the only option in a small community, how easy is it to get child care? There will be mothers who want to go out to work, and others who want to offer a child-care service, but from where comes the encouragement and support for this to happen?

How does it become viable if there are only two or three young children in a small village, and mothers start and stop work at different times? How do the local services make sure there is provision? How can nursery vouchers apply to small child-care units and how do we make it easy for employers, employees and child carers, and thereby allow women to play a full part in their community?

We know how important women are to our communities – voluntary work on children's parties, senior citizen parties, gala days, fitness clubs, the list goes on – and their contribution could be even greater if they had the level of support and peace of mind to know that their children are safe and happy while they are at work.

The impact of the social responsibility remit of the then Highlands and Islands Development Board was clearly felt in our home. My mother was one of the founders of Scalpay Isle Knitwear in the late 1960s. The island of Scalpay was thriving at this time. The HIDB's support for the fishing community had brought new fishing boats and prosperity because of ring-net fishing for herring. While the fishing was a fantastic boon to the island, there was hardly any paid employment for women. There wasn't, and still isn't, a hotel on Scalpay. A car-ferry had just arrived, but with the kind of timetable that made it impossible to live on Scalpay and do any kind of meaningful day job, except teaching, on mainland Harris.

However, every woman in Scalpay knew how to knit. We were never allowed to be idle as young girls. My mother claimed you could do simple knitting, such as socks, and read a book at the same time. With great encouragement from Bob Storey and Calum R Morrison from HIDB, a small group of women set up Scalpay Isle Knitwear. It was never a great commercial success, but it lasted for over 20 years and she loved it.

My mother loved the sense of purpose in helping many talented knitters get more money for their work. She loved their annual trip to Aviemore for the Highland Trade Fair. But most of all she loved the camaraderie among women as they gathered once or twice a week to process orders, invoices and payments. The financial reward for the work was probably less than £1 an hour, but that didn't detract from their sense of fulfilment and wellbeing at working together and getting a better price and recognition for their and others' labour.

We have creative and entrepreneurial women working in all our islands and in many remote areas in between. Enabling and encouraging women to have fulfilling employment should be a priority for all our public services, and it should be a focus for the services to work together to achieve this. What we are talking about are micro policies, where provision may only impact on one or two families. However, making it available is crucial, both to the women's wellbeing and sense of confidence and to ensuring that a local community can fully exploit all the talent that is available to it.

By looking seriously at supporting child care at a micro level you provide not only employment for women looking for a safe and nurturing place for their children, but also an opportunity for others to develop a career in child care. Given the availability of broadband, there are so many ways in which technology can be exploited to allow girls and women to study and acquire qualifications and develop their own independence, all of which creates confidence. A confident woman nurtures a confident child, who in turn helps to ensure a confident community.

There is evidence that women, especially women with young children, have less confidence at work than do men, and therefore building confidence is vital. I had some direct experience in the past few years when, for a short time, I was involved in running a charity and social enterprise in Skye.

When I took over, all key decisions were taken in the Edinburgh office which, rather than fulfil its remit of supporting the operation on Skye, had completely changed the dynamics of power, simply because the chief executive was based in Edinburgh. There was a patronising attitude towards the team in Skye, which impacted negatively on the team's sense of itself and its motivation. It became clear to me very early on that there was enormous skill and talent available to the organization, but little self-belief. It did not take much investment of time and listening to help change attitudes and build confidence.

Lack of empathy and understanding can very quickly crush people, and what might start off as reticence quickly becomes a lack of self-belief. Coupled with patronage at best and contempt at worst, it doesn't take long for people to become de-energised and demotivated. I am delighted that many in that organization, and most of them are women, are now in promoted posts, and that the organization is doing very well.

The Money

Where there is talk of significant empowerment, budgets need to reflect the cost of implementation and sustainability. Building thriving rural communities has its price. Investment, if managed creatively, and by that I don't mean unaccountably, will pay off across all areas of public spending for many generations. Engagement leads to a sense of physical and mental wellbeing, which in turn puts less pressure on our health and social services and creates greater value all round, which is why it is important to look at investment across the board rather than within each agency's budget.

I welcomed, and I am still supportive of, the concept of the Curriculum for Excellence, which was introduced to Scottish schools in 2010. Its ambition to enable young people to become successful learners, confident individuals, responsible citizens and effective contributors was and still is laudable. The emphasis on the physical and mental wellbeing of every child, including being respected and having a sense of belonging, cannot be over-estimated.

How many people do we know who hated school and who couldn't bear the sarcasm and cruelty of teachers with contempt for all but the most academic pupils? So many wasted their young lives learning very little because of fear of being ridiculed, and consequent feelings of inferiority and worthlessness. Part of the vision of the Curriculum for Excellence was to do away with all of that, and by so doing close the attainment gap which is all too prevalent in Scottish schools.

The reason it has not succeeded is that there was not enough investment in its implementation. All visions and strategies are worthless, unless the planning for implementation is robust and supported by sufficient funding to ensure that the change is managed and that people are trained and supported properly to embrace and own the change. Unless commitment to action is uncompromised, the rhetoric is worthless.

The problem with the Curriculum for Excellence was that teachers were not trained properly, there was not enough consultation about how the vision would play out in the classroom, and not enough listening to, or allaying of, teachers' concerns. And, of course, there was the insatiable appetite to collect data and to keep checking up. Like all professionals, teachers who are motivated and experienced will respond with enthusiasm to the needs and circumstances of their pupils. They are much more likely to be motivated by the child in front of them than by completing yet another form on their computer screen.

Learning to Live Here

Our understanding of how children learn is now so much better than it was when my generation was seated in serried rows being talked at, or often shouted at. A greater underpinning of children's relationship with, and pride in, their own community and environment could do so much to address the population decline and the demographic deficit that is still such a threat to our most peripheral communities. If educational success was coupled with staying rather than with leaving, what a great story our schools could tell.

A strong understanding of our local environment, learned in school, also has the potential to provide the basis for one of the most important elements of our economy: tourism. We encounter sophisticated travellers almost every day who are interested in our heritage, history, environment and culture. We are also much better at responding to these opportunities, but how much easier if we were encouraged to take a deep interest in our own community from a very early age?

The development of the University of the Highlands and Islands makes it easier to study in our own communities, but there is much more to be done to develop the robustness of Broadband and internet access to ensure that all technological tools are available and at our disposal. There is much made of lifelong learning, but to be to be full participants in lifelong learning we need the tools: like reliable and adequate Broadband access and speed.

Broadband and mobile phone signals are as significant to our infrastructure as transport. However, one does not negate the other. While communications networks are vital, equally important are reliable and affordable transport links. Ferries and their timetables must be fit for purpose, air services must be adequately resourced to ensure reliability, and roads and railways must be maintained to make travel as reliable as possible.

It was clear last summer that the infrastructure of the west Highlands and Islands was under severe pressure. An encounter with three camper vans coming up or going down the Quirang or the Bealach was not for the faint-hearted. Finding adequate toilets or even passing places was often a challenge. There has been much hand-wringing about the challenges, but very little action to my knowledge, and this year's visitor influx is not so far away.

While initiatives like Road Equivalent Tariff (a way of calculating subsidy on island-mainland sea journeys, which reduces the cost of the voyage to passengers to the same as an equivalent mileage by road) on ferry fares are welcome, a 2013 study by HIE shows that those living in our remotest areas need to spend 40 per cent more than those living in urban areas to have a minimum living standard. This is a significant sum, given that salaries in the remoter areas are often lower than average. It is not just the cost of travel that needs to be addressed, it is also the cost of freight and the additional penalty imposed for delivering to remoter postcodes.

And then there is our health service. Recently, the Western Isles Health Board highlighted the challenge of an ageing workforce alongside recruitment problems. NHS Highland has been completely at odds with the residents of North Skye over hospital provision, and there is ongoing concern at the lack of a permanent district nurse on Raasay: examples of how local needs are far from being met. There is also the problem that district nurses are now not responsible for children under 16. This is the domain of the health visitor, as I understand it.

This type of policy may be fine for big centres of populations, but hardly sensible for this part of the world. Perhaps an additional qualification is all that is needed, or surely basic nursing skills in an emergency should suffice? It is difficult to ascertain whether it is a problem of recruitment or funding, but Raasay must have a district nurse. How do families, young or old, feel comfortable living on an island knowing that medical care is at best a ferry ride away?

In Scalpay of my youth, Agnes, the nurse, was the health service on the island. She was the first point of call, was highly skilled, often made life and death decisions, and everyone had complete confidence in her. When a boat had to be launched, and the only doctor in North Harris called to make the crossing, she knew the importance of the best use of resource. I don't think I ever heard anyone voicing concern about the level of health care in my youth. Perhaps expectations were not so high then, but in many rural areas confidence in the local health service is diminishing.

The alternative offered to residents of Raasay is that the emergency services, in this case coastguard, helicopter, ferry or lifeboat, will be called into service if needed. However, were there to be a holistic approach to public expenditure, it wouldn't take many emergency callouts to exceed the cost of having a permanent nurse on the island. Effective medical provision is an absolute must if the confidence that has started to build is to be sustained.

As our Community Land Trusts have developed, and as we see a reversal of decline and a rise in confidence in some of these areas, it is obvious that decision-making should be as close as possible to the grassroots. Public servants should see their role as cheerleaders and advocates for these communities. HIE's understanding of its role has gone a long way along that road, although there is no room for complacency.

I remember a conversation I had in the late 1970s with an official from the HIDB. Ring-net herring fishing was in decline and the building of factories like Breascleit and Ardveenish was based on a vision that the local fishermen would go for fishing boats with a greater catching capacity and costing much more to run. The official was scathing about fishermen in the Western Isles who were choosing smaller boats and creel fishing. He thought they were lazy and unambitious. As time has shown, this was the sensible thing to do. If the HIDB had been in listening mode at the time, it could have helped to create greater value at the pier head, encouraged hotels and restaurants to use local produce much earlier, and helped to continue a vibrant fishing industry.

The response to a 'one size fits all' in this instance was an opportunity lost. Luckily, there were a few enterprises like Kallin Seafoods in Grimsay which have survived and thrived, because they had the vision and the ability to implement and develop a sustainable enterprise, despite the prevailing official view of the time.

Creating the Vision

There is evidence that, for workforces, autonomy and responsibility go hand in hand with the most successful companies and organisations. This means that the role of boards and senior management teams is to create a culture in which people can give of their best. In other words, not micro-manage tasks, but rather create the vision and then the environment to motivate and inspire people. The other piece of evidence is that senior managers who listen and are closely attuned to their workforce are always more successful than those who don't.

There is no doubt that, over the years, HIE has been listening and is much better at scaling and understanding local need. Its 'Strengthening Communities' approach looks beyond the practices of the past to genuine capacity building for the future.

The key elements of the Communities Regeneration Act are local initiatives where people identify issues and opportunities in their local area, and decide what to do about them to make positive changes. It also empowers people to call public servants to account which, in our remoter areas, makes it important for our elected representatives to understand why joining the dots at local level is much more important than exporting accountability to Edinburgh.

And we need a better way of accounting for the public purse to accommodate specific needs, rather than the other way around: economies of service delivery for the remoter communities being forced into the straitjacket of urban policies.

At all levels, there must be a focus on micro solutions, which create as much intellectual and logistical challenge as big projects, but that is how it should be. I know it is early days for The Harris Distillery, but the recent BBC Alba series, 'Dileag Na Hearadh', was inspiring in highlighting how the confidence of the team increased over the year. Being part of an ambitious project, and obviously being much respected and having interesting work every day, is so motivating and encouraging that the results are obvious.

A continuing commitment to a holistic approach is the only way that smaller and remote communities will thrive. Policy for rural areas must start with need. That is why HIE has a specific social role. Solutions for rural areas will not fit templates and policies which are drawn up for urban areas or large centres of population.

While much progress has been made over the past 50 years, the overall problem of depopulation and ageing communities has not gone away. It is time for our political representatives to be bold and to build on what has been achieved. It is time to become much more accountable to the electorate, rather than toeing the party line.

With ingenuity, partnering and initiative from our public servants, there could be a way of building on community initiatives, ensuring prudent spending, transparency and accountability by bringing resources together at local level rather than governance at national level.

We have taken great steps since the re-organisation of local government in 1975 but, in areas where the problems of depopulation and an ageing demographic are acute, there must be a radical approach. I suggest that, rather than government concerning itself with governance at a national level, it instead sets about establishing levers for accountability at a local level – the appraisals done by those who are most impacted by the policies, rather than by quango kings and queens.

That would keep all of us on our toes.

Afterword

Iain MacDonald

This book was written and produced during the first three months of 2017, following the announcement in November 2016 by Deputy First Minister John Swinney of the Scottish government's plans for HIE, as well as Scottish Enterprise, Skills Development Scotland and the Scottish Funding Council.

On 18 January 2017, the government's intentions for HIE were defeated in the Holyrood chamber by a single vote. In February, a report drawn up for the government by HIE chair Lorne Crerar proposed that HIE should keep a 'delivery board', still subordinate to a centrally based authority.

On 1 March 2017, the part of the plan affecting the abolition of the Scottish Funding Council's board was also defeated in the parliament, once again by a single vote. On 7 March, the Northern Isles Liberal Democrat MSP Tavish Scott claimed that his attempt to obtain all internal ministerial and official communications on HIE had been rejected by the government as failing the 'public interest test'. He appealed to the Scottish Information Commissioner.

At the time of writing, the Scottish government is promising a statement will be made on the entire issue 'in the coming weeks'. By the time you hold this book in your hands, it's possible that this will have happened. But the lessons from this controversy are clear, whatever the future of Highlands and Islands Enterprise.

There were good reasons for establishing HIDB, and for its remit for both social and economic development. These reasons are well rehearsed in earlier chapters of this book. They still exist, in particular in outlying parts of the Highlands and Islands.

It was once considered that a social dimension was essential for any public body active in the Highlands. That was true, for instance, in the activities of the Forestry Commission in the north. The recognition of the area's special circumstances was included also in the constitution of the North of Scotland Hydro-Electric Board which, as the name suggests, produced power from the glens – but also reasonably-priced power *to* the glens, under the leadership of Tom Johnston.

The Hydro Board was privatised in 1991 and later, when it merged with Southern Electric, became Scottish and Southern Energy. Today, how many consumers of SSE power remember that it used to be the Highlands' own electric company and that it once had a social responsibility included in its constitution?

John Swinney's intention to 'declutter' the Scottish public sector skyline aims for a more streamlined Scotland. But, in recent years, what that has meant is a slow dilution of HIE's role and influence in bringing Highlands and Islands solutions to Highlands and Islands problems, perhaps intended to prepare it for a seamless merging with other agencies with different problems.

The SNP government has in the past recognised the different nature of places like the Western Isles, for instance, where they introduced Road Equivalent Tariff, a subsidy formula which has reduced the cost of sea travel to and from the islands to that of the equivalent journey by road.

That's been good for the islands' economy, though the government, bafflingly, elected not to apply it to freight operators. It's worth noting that RET was most enthusiastically promoted to successive governments by HIE.

The SNP, in seeking to consolidate its credentials as a competent party of government, appears to believe that the best way to do this is to take direct control of as many agencies and other quangos as possible, in order to have a streamlined Scotland.

The language it applies to this vision, though, is not calculated to inspire. In a paper to the Convention of the Highlands and Islands, the government outlined its aims for HIE and the other agencies: 'This will involve the creation of an overarching, strategic board for Scotland's enterprise and skills agencies to drive hard alignment of services and strategic goals to tackle Scotland's long-term economic challenges and deliver on all 4 pillars of Scotland's Economic Strategy'. It would, said ministers (or possibly civil servants), 'utilise a strong industry and wider stakeholder voice to help shape our collective impact and effectiveness in transforming productivity, driving a step change in the performance of our economy, and delivering strong, vibrant and inclusive growth at scale'.

Contrast this with the bold, buccaneering vision of Robert Grieve in HIDB's first Annual Report. Perhaps more than the language has changed.

In an earlier chapter in this book, James Hunter suggests that 'change' means returning the Highlands and Islands to pre-1886 conditions. That would be a dreadful legacy, all in pursuit of something called 'hard alignment'.

Scotland has been living with devolution since last century. Independence need not be the enemy of devolution within Scotland. And one size, no matter how much decluttering goes on, will never remotely fit all.

Iain MacDonald, March 2017